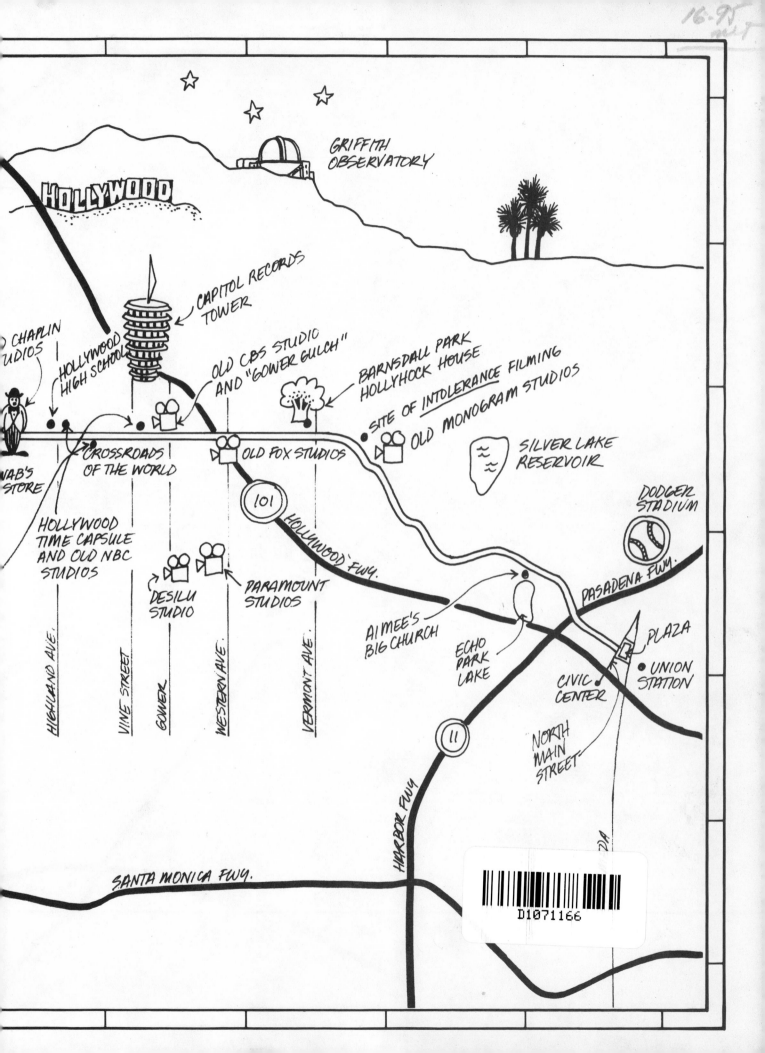

16-95
M.T.

D1071166

AMERICA'S DREAM STREET

JOE KENNELLEY
&
ROY HANKEY

DARWIN PUBLICATIONS/BURBANK, CALIFORNIA

darwin publications
850 N. Hollywood Way · Burbank, California 91505

ISBN 0-933506-06-6

Printed in the United States of America.

ACKNOWLEDGEMENTS

Our journey down Sunset Boulevard could not have been made without the help of Carl S. Fleming, Variety Arts Center; Dave Alpert, A&M Records; Francis and George F. Montgomery; Gerry Dixon; Betty Ellison, California Room, Los Angeles Public Library; Zola Clearwater; Walter Rogala; Keith Schroeder; William Pugsley; David Valenzuela; Desirée Kennelley; and Joanne Sendy Katz.

Unless otherwise credited, all photos are by Roy Hankey.

TABLE OF CONTENTS

PREFACE

While talking with friends at Schwab's, a prominent Hollywood producer once remarked, "Sunset Boulevard—it's America's dream street, you know." He may not have known that Mary Pickford had called it "the street of dreams and hopes," while Charlie Chaplin once said quite simply, "I used to live on that great boulevard."

It seems there has always been a Sunset Boulevard. Who, on hearing the name, doesn't conjure images of a wide, uninterrupted road lined with lovely mansions, neatly edged lawns and flower beds, spectacular high rises, low-and-wide pastel edifices, quaint store fronts with Hansel-and-Gretel or English tea-room facades, splendid hotels and restaurants, and parks bordered with magnificent tall palms? Who doesn't think of "77 Sunset Strip" or Gloria Swanson's *Sunset Boulevard*, or the stately Beverly Hills Hotel, where dwelled such shining stars as Marlene Dietrich, William Powell, Marion Davies, Maurice Chevalier, John Barrymore, Douglas Fairbanks, Sr., and Norma Talmadge, just for starters? How many star-gazers and star-hopefuls have, through the decades, strolled along Sunset near Vine Street or out on "the Strip", longing for a glimpse of their favorite idol (or *any* star, for that matter!) so they might regale the folks back home with the happy coincidence?

Along this road some of the first "moving picture factories" were erected, later to become the highly sophisticated motion picture studios. Hollywood's pioneers cleared weeded lots to establish their businesses, and sliced the lower slopes of the Hollywood Hills to build their first homes. Then came other industries and, inevitably, the fantastic real estate boom. Why, one could buy a lovely lot with a hundred-foot frontage in the Echo Park district for a paltry sixty dollars, while out in West Los Angeles, beyond La Brea Avenue, fifty feet of handsome boulevard frontage could be snatched up for a mere $300.

Sunset Boulevard is a picture of contrasts — ugly in places, even trashy; in other places long stretches of middle-class mediocrity, and farther westward, mansions with panoramas of manicured lawns and sprawling gardens with vibrant hues. This twenty-seven-mile-long avenue was originally several streets linked together over a fifty-five-year span. But it seemed always to be there—as an unconscious need, or as a conscious dream. Haven't most of us imagined that someday, some way, after all our dreams had come true, we'd be sublimely dwelling in a great house on such a splendid boulevard?

We've prepared this book in seven sections: In the Beginning — The Plaza; Echo Park — Ethnic Mix and Aimee's Big Church; Hollywood — One Reelers to Color T.V.; The Strip — Sunset's Golden Era; Beverly Hills — The Money Kingdom; Bel-Air/Brentwood — The Boulevard's Suburban Paradise; and, Pacific Palisades — End of the Yellow Brick Road. In these we've striven to evoke an historical spirit, to touch upon some nostalgic chords, to scan the past and take a look at today. It has been said that we've hit upon a sort of legendary countenance in the process of linking these sections together. Many people, many events, many circumstances have made Sunset Boulevard into a memorable street. At its best and at its worst, from its east end at the Plaza to its abrupt demise at the shores of the Pacific, this great boulevard remains one of the most fabulous thoroughfares in all the world.

1

IN THE BEGINNING
The Plaza

It all began where a dusty cow trail about twenty-five feet wide wended its way from a sloping pasture just west of the Plaza into the tiny settlement of El Pueblo de Los Angeles where eleven families had settled a year earlier. They had come from Mission San Gabriel Archangel about nine miles away, led by Felipe de Neve. This tall Mexican army officer, serving as Mexican California's provisional governor, had been ordered to establish a settlement on the west bank of the Rio Porcuincula, where corn and a variety of vegetables would be grown. Apparently, the objective was to "plant the seeds" of a future town, for the town to be self-sufficient, for it to initiate barter with other California settlements and to become, in time, the trade center for surrounding ranchos and their colonies of vaqueros, leather craftsmen, ironsmiths, carpenters, and tile makers.

That was back in 1781. The cow trail appeared after the eleven families — Sonorans and Sinaloans — each had been given a few head of cattle, some seeds, young grapevines, tools and certain other provisions. Two of the families put their cows to pasture on the slope just west of the settlement, and here, unpredictably, began the tiny street that developed into glamorous Sunset Boulevard. There were other cow trails, too, south and east of the settlement. About twenty years later these trails had become narrow roads that meandered through the town or went down to the river's edge. A few ran in a straight line; others wound aimlessly around adobe houses, plank sheds and lean-to chicken coops. By 1840, following a swelling influx of immigrants from the East and Midwest, a few of the wider, more often used streets were given names. Mexican *carretas* creaked along *Calle Principal* ("Main Street"), *Calle de Las Esperanzas* ("Street of Hopes"), *Calle de Caridad* ("Street of Charity"), *Calle de Chapules* ("Street of Grasshoppers"), and *Calle de San Pedro* ("Street of Saint Peter"). Little un-named streets proliferated. The business district and the budding residential area hugging the Plaza — a central "park" where de Neve first read the proclamation establishing the settlement — still had nameless, winding streets by 1849. That year territorial governor General Bennet Riley, upon requesting a map of Los Angeles from the town's *ayuntamiento*, discovered that nobody had ever bothered to draw one.

Within sixty days an army surveyor was summoned to plot the city. Nameless trails and streets were named. Some areas were partitioned into lots; others were designated as gardens, corn fields, or plowed and unplowed land. Street names were shown in both English and Spanish. In a few instances, according to this first map, a house or store would be indicated right in the middle of the street! The surveyor made Main Street run through Sixth Street. Fort Street dead-ended at the edge of an orange grove, and High Street shot northward into a tiny section called Sonoratown, where most of the Sonoran immigrants had settled into what probably was Los Angeles' first ghetto. Up cropped Chinatown, a gathering of huts, hovels, shacks, one-room adobes, and small stores built by Chinese immigrants who'd worked the mines around Randsburg and Johannesburg in the Mojave Desert and in mining settlements in Northern California, and who had now come to Los Angeles in search of jobs or peaceful retirement.

But where was Sunset? In 1859 the committee assigned by the *ayuntamiento* to "square the plaza" opened up an avenue to the north. Formerly known as Upper Main, it cut through several shacks and stuccos. An appendage of this street ran off to the right in an easterly direction, coming to a dead-end at the edge of Chinatown, barely 600 feet from Upper Main. There was something historically prophetic in this simple straight line on the map. *This was the beginning of Sunset Boule-*

vard. Although no one could possibly have conceived the future of this narrow road, it gradually began to grow into an avenue that would one day pass through five Southern California communities and stretch to the white sands of the Pacific Ocean twenty-seven miles away. It would become one of the most famous streets in America — indeed, the whole world — through books, periodicals, films, television, and word-of-mouth.

That embryonic 600 feet, which a year later pushed into Chinatown to couple with that district's "main walk" had rudimentary structures facing its north side within a matter of two years. The south end of famous Olvera Street — Los Angeles' first street to branch off the Plaza — touched upon this 600-foot strip and ended on Macy Street to the north. And thus it remained almost unchanged for another thirty years. At that time the city fathers extended the appendage westward to meet a Catholic orphanage being built "on the edge of town almost in the fields," and connected it to a short, primitive road called Childs Avenue. A year later it was linked to a short, curved path which used to be called Douglas Walk, probably the origin of today's curving Douglas Street.

As Los Angeles grew, its citizens spread westward into the gentle hills, following dirt roads evolved from wagon and *carreta* trails coming in from outlying farms. These roads often took the names of the nearest farm. Winding trails at the foot of the hills took on names, too. Eventually, in 1888, this expanding "boulevard" connected with portions of Elysian Avenue and Effie Street, which were to become main thoroughfares of early Echo Park. That same year some unknown but imaginative civic employee, probably in the city's planning office, named this boulevard "Sunset" — perhaps because when a traveler left the Plaza and went westward he rode or walked into the afternoon sun.

The new Sunset Boulevard then crossed a road called Logan Street, today a busy crossroad in the heart of Echo Park. It was not far from this point that wise city fathers later ordered Sunset to be cut through a hill so travelers needn't make a sharp curve around it — good planning, they believed, for the town's primary modes of transportation: the horse and buggy and that new-fangled contraption, the "auto-mobile".

These same city fathers, while fretting over a direct passage through a pesky hill couldn't possibly have imagined that near this same hill would evolve a populous suburb boasting a scrambled mix of no less than a dozen ethnic groups, a suburb that would create a placid, palm-fringed lake for its delight, and that someday, on the lake's green shores, would host the fiery super-evangelist, Aimee Semple McPherson and her renowned Angelus Temple of the Foursquare Gospel. Echo Park, a sylvan scene barely two miles west of the old Plaza, embraced Sunset Boulevard, and the little community spread rapidly up the grassy hillsides toward the setting sun.

The Plaza where Los Angeles — and Sunset Boulevard — began, photographed around 1876 from Fort Moore Hill to the west. The original tip of what was to become Sunset Boulevard departs from the broad pathway to the left of the circle of shrubs. At the far side of the circle is the Vincente Lugo Townhouse, given to the church, opposite, for a school. St. Vincent's College, later Loyola University, started here. Today Union Station sits in the field directly behind the school. [Title Insurance and Trust Company] □

Looking north on Chinatown's *Calle de los Negros*, around 1882. Chinatown sprawled adjacent to the eastern end of Sunset, near where the Boulevard began. In the background, left, is the old fire station and tower. [Title Insurance and Trust Company] □

6

Castelar Street, looking north
into Sonoratown around 1890,
photographed from the northwest
corner of Sunset. Today's
Chinatown, relocated in the
1930s to make way for Union
Station, begins about a block
down this street. [Title Insurance
and Trust Company] □

A Chinatown festival around
1905. [Los Angeles Public
Library] □

The main entrance to Union Station, built in 1939. Beneath the building a maze of secret tunnels and dungeons dug by Chinese inhabitants from about 1870 to 1930 were discovered by construction crews. □

Across the street from Union Station, the Plaza takes on a festive air. □

Union Station's beautiful lobby shows its Spanish cathedral influence. The spacious depot, which occupies part of the original Chinatown, was practically deserted after Los Angeles International Airport opened in 1950. [Union Pacific Railroad] □

Sailors disembark from troop trains at Union Station during World War II to merge into the weekend crowds on Sunset Boulevard. Most of these men headed for the Hollywood Canteen, then on to the Sunset Strip. [Union Pacific Railroad] □

This statue of Father Junipero Serra was originally set on an island in the middle of Sunset Boulevard, but was moved in 1969 to make way for a remodeling of the Plaza, during which about 1,000 feet of Sunset were removed. A replica of the original housed in Washington, D.C., the statue now adorns the Plaza. □

The old Lugo residence in 1886, after having been converted to a Chinese restaurant. Some descendants of the Lugo family still live near downtown Los Angeles. [Title Insurance and Trust Company] □

The old fire station, below, right, housing "Fire Truck Number One" and the restored Garnier Building, to its left. These old structures stand near the foot of Sunset Boulevard. Los Angeles City Hall is in the background, left. □

Ready for horses to be hitched, old "Fire Truck Number One" waits to fight conflagration. This station, housing the historic wagon, equipment, and the only firehouse turntable in the country, faces the Plaza. The last fire horse ran in 1929. □
Below, the Plaza today, looking northeast from the City Hall tower. The rear of the Pico House and Garnier Building are at the lower left. Beyond the Garnier Building is the fire station. Union Station is near the center, and the huge building to the left of center is the Post Office Terminal Annex. □

A vendor's stand in the Plaza serves local patrons and visitors from afar. □

The lovely Mercedes Theatre, the first in Los Angeles, was built against the rear wall of the Pico House hotel. The smaller building at right is the first Masonic Hall in Los Angeles. □ Below, the famous Pico House as it appeared in 1875. Designed and furnished by Pio Pico himself, it was the first three-story building in Los Angeles. It still stands at North Main and Sanchez Streets, a short walk from Sunset Boulevard. [Los Angeles Public Library] □

The Plaza church in 1870.
A small cemetery is at left under the trees. ☐
The church in 1876, with a new cemetery wall and the Cape House Restaurant beyond. The cross no longer tops the church's gable. ☐

18

By 1904 the mission-style bell tower has replaced the cupola, the cemetery is gone, and there are additional buildings on the hillside. □ The church's interior, photographed in 1957. [All four, Los Angeles Public Library] □

EL CAMINO REAL
NUESTRA SEÑORA LA REINA
DE LOS ANGELES
FOUNDED 1784-RESTORED 1861

Commemorative bells placed by the California State Department of Parks and Recreation mark the route of Father Junipero Serra and his missionaries. □

Founder's Cross at the entrance to Olvera Street, below Sunset Boulevard. Spanish army officer Felipe de Neve was sent by the Mission Padres to "begin and lay out a pueblo" with a group of Mexican and Negro families on the western bank of what is now the Los Angeles River. □

21

Historic Olvera Street. The brick structure on the left is one of the oldest buildings still standing in Los Angeles. Built as a residence in the early 1870s, it now serves as a store and warehouse. West of this *avenida* lay a narrow cow trail later widened and named "Sunset Street." □

Below, the famous Avila House, first "permanent" residence in the pueblo of Los Angeles. From 1846 to 1847 it served as headquarters of the conquering Yankee battalion when it seized the town from the Californios — native Californians who considered themselves neither Mexicans nor Americans. Four families subsequently owned the house until it was turned into an historical monument by the City of Los Angeles. □

The main bedroom of the
Avila House on Olvera Street,
said to be the first street
branching off from the Plaza. The
cow trail later named Sunset
came within 200 feet of this old
adobe, built by one of the first
settlers in Los Angeles. □

A weekend in the Plaza. □

The Blessing of the Animals, an annual event held at the Plaza a week before Easter. The tradition originated in remembrance of St. Francis of Assisi. □

A 1920 view of the northwest corner of Spring Street at Sunset Boulevard in what was originally Sonoratown. Note the awning and billboard in Spanish. [Los Angeles Public Library] □

The Fort Hill Monument near the Plaza. The Inscription reads: "On this site stood Fort Moore built by the Mormon Battalion during the War With Mexico....The Flag of the United States was raised here on July 4th, 1847." Fort Moore overlooked the Plaza, Sonoratown to the north, and the trail which became Sunset Boulevard. □

The northwest corner of North Broadway and Sunset in 1910. The downtown Pacific Electric Express train left this terminal for Venice and Redondo-by-the-Sea, now known as Redondo Beach. [Southern California Edison Company/Interurbans Publications] □

Below, the driver of the wagon on Sunset Boulevard near the Plaza surely never imagined that what was a quiet little road in 1886 would one day be a grand thoroughfare teeming with horseless machines competing for

space, bumper-to-bumper, at unheard-of speeds. On the knoll in the center is the home of J. W. Robinson, department store tycoon. [Title Insurance and Trust Company] □

The J. W. Robinson home in 1890. [Los Angeles Public Library] □

The bottom photo was taken from a 1905 edition of an Italian magazine writing about the "Regina Coeli Asylum," a convent and orphanage for Italian and Spanish children in Los Angeles. J.W. Robinson's widow Julia turned the home over to the Missionary Sisters of the Sacred Heart, headed by Mother Frances Cabrini, canonized as a Saint in 1946. The once-sacred grounds of Mother Cabrini eventually became a haven for derelicts and the property was demolished in 1973. [Missionary Sisters of the Sacred Heart] □

REGINA COELI ASYLUM LOS ANGELES CAL.
MISSIONARY SISTERS OF THE SACRED HEART.

In the top photo, the Mother Cabrini-J.W. Robinson knoll is at the left and Sunset Boulevard is in the foreground. Lights from Dodger Stadium appear on the rim of the hill, upper left. Chinatown occupies the center and upper right. □

A festive air always seems to adorn "New Chinatown" near Castelar Street, off Sunset. □

Remains of a shrine still stand on the vacant grounds of Mother Cabrini's orphan asylum. Cabrini's Missionary Sisters of the Sacred Heart celebrated their 100th anniversary in 1980. □ Below, townspeople gather for the public hanging of the bandit Lachenais, who dangles between the open gates, just off Sunset Boulevard near downtown Los Angeles, in June of 1870. It is believed this lynching took place alongside Temple Street and that the hill in the background is the present-day site of the Los Angeles Music Center [Title Insurance and Trust Company] □

Part of Fort Moore Hill as it is today, looking south on Grand, formerly Charity Street. The Lower cross street is Sunset. The Music Center's Dorothy Chandler Pavillion (circular building) is at Temple Street. □

One of the few remaining
Sunset Boulevard homes in the
Figueroa area, built around
1900. Original construction cost:
about $2,500! □

The downtown Los Angeles skyline glitters above the busy interchange of the Harbor-Pasadena and Hollywood Freeways at the Sunset Boulevard overpass. The Plaza where Sunset began is nearby.
□

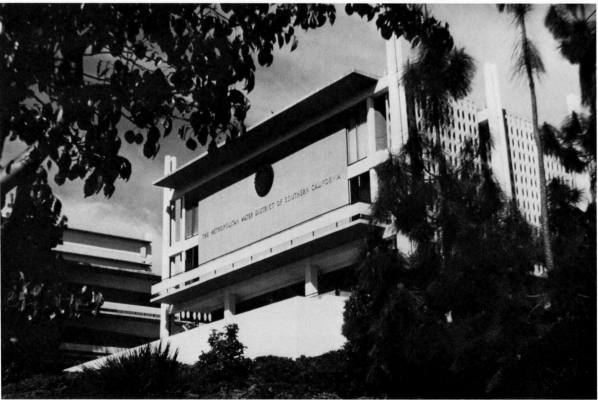

The Los Angeles Infirmary, on Sunset at Beaudry Park, in 1888. Sisters Hospital took it over in 1898 and it eventually became the original site of St. Vincent's Hospital. [Los Angeles Public Library] ☐
Today the general offices of the Metropolitan Water District of Southern California occupy this exact spot. ☐

The south portal of the old Hill Street tunnel cut in 1909. The tunnel extended Hill Street towards Sunset, but no longer exists. (This view is often mistaken for the Third Street and Hill tunnel, still in use.) [Southern California Edison Company/Interurbans Publications] □

Below, the north portal of the 1909 Hill Street tunnel. [Interurbans Publications] □

ECHO PARK
Ethnic Mix and Aimee's Big Church

Nobody seems to know why Aimee Semple McPherson chose the Echo Park district to make a home for herself and her orphaned daughter, Roberta, who was only eight years old when the pair arrived in Los Angeles in 1918. Off Lemoyne Street, near Echo Park Lake, she rented a one-bedroom house, after riding out Sunset from the old railway station in downtown Los Angeles. She had just completed a transcontinental gospel tour, preaching in tents and auditoriums all the way from Providence, Rhode Island. Los Angeles was to be her last stop. She'd accumulated nearly $2,000 and three trunkloads of clothing along the way. Her mother and a friend, Essie Binkley, also an evangelist, persuaded Aimee to settle in Los Angeles. No more wandering.

"This is a new frontier for God's work," they told her, and she believed it. Los Angeles was booming. From the Midwest and East people flocked to the sunny hills and beaches of Southern California, and to the jobs opening up everywhere. Aimee could see that there was money in this land of promise — and thousands of sinners needing God. She set up headquarters on Lemoyne Street with her mother and Essie Binkley as her assistants. In 1922, after holding forty giant revivals in Los Angeles and other cities in sixteen states, Aimee plunked down $5,000 cash and applied for a loan to build a "temple of evangelism" to bring people into the "loving arms of Jesus." The impressive structure was erected across a narrow street from the lake that attracted Sunday sightseers and families out for weekend picnics. Sunset Boulevard was only a block away and, as they passed, folks spotted the shining dome, glistening concrete walls, and the silvery aluminum-coated tar paper roof.

The little community of Echo Park grew rapidly after the first houses were built in the late 1870s, nestling snugly along hidden lanes that ribbon the hills overlooking Sunset. Below the Boulevard, where the hills become gentle knolls, Aimee's temple stood gloriously among the old wooden and stucco cottages that dotted narrow dirt roads leading southwestward toward Alvarado Street. On New Year's Day, 1923, Aimee threw open her temple doors, following an advertisement she had placed in the *Los Angeles Examiner*. Within four months 7,000 men, women and children were seeking salvation at Aimee's altar; of those, 1,200 were immersed in baptismal waters.

The multitudes heeding Aimee's call were not the only ones to descend upon the area. Hundreds of immigrant families in search of low-rent apartments or cheap lots on which to build houses decided to make Echo Park their home. Situated halfway between central Los Angeles and Hollywood, and near the northern tip of Alvarado Street — a main artery to the vineyards and walnut groves to the south — Echo Park became a hub for immigrant settlers seeking jobs of all kinds. There were merchants and small factories in downtown Los Angeles, movie studios in Hollywood, and small farms southward in the Crenshaw, Culver City and Griffith Ranch areas.

First came the German and Russian families; following them, the Swedes. Poles and Hungarians came next; then Orientals. And, of course, the Mexican families — third-generation descendants of earlier Plaza settlers — were already there. These immigrants built the "town" of Echo Park. The clusters of small stores and cafes, the tiny bungalows and apartment houses grouped at the corners of Sunset and Lemoyne, and Echo Park Avenue, were mainly owned by this community of immigrants — all good neighbors living quiet suburban lives, watching the growing stream of people traveling out Sunset, and profiting from them as they paused at the beautiful lake.

Against the hills the more affluent families built two-story "California Bungalows" — some stuccoed in soft pastels, with large roofed porches and arbor-covered patios, and others made of wood, with shingled siding and hints of Oriental design. In the late 1920s art festivals were held on the lake's shores, where artists and art-goers shared picnic lunches on the lawn. Eager vendors set up lemonade stands on Sunset to offer refreshments to the visitors getting off streetcars, while Aimee's people passed out religious pamphlets and invited them inside for prayer meetings. Some of the out-of-area artists remained in Echo Park and thus the first art "colony" in Southern California was born. Today a remaining handful of outstanding California artists maintain their homes and studios in the hills just above Sunset. One of these is Leo Politi.

A few movie stars in the late twenties also made their homes in Echo Park, in preference to the newer, more fashionable neighborhoods of Hollywood and Beverly Hills. Among these were Gilbert Roland, character actor Morris Ankrum, Lupe Velez, comedian Oliver Hardy, and silent screen director-producer Mack Sennett. Fatty Arbuckle spent his last years here, and in 1979 his widow died in a small Sunset Boulevard house on Echo Park's western end, approaching the Silver Lake region.

Other residents, recent or current, include famous screenwriters Gloria Katz and Willard Huyck; novelist Roger Simon, author of the Moses Wine detective stories; Leonard Weinglass, attorney for the "Chicago Seven" and Bill and Emily Harris of the Patricia Hearst kidnapping; musician-composer Jackson Browne; legal entrepreneur Art Goldberg; and journalist Liza Williams. The adjacent Silver Lake neighborhood is or has been home to California Governor Edmund G. Brown, Jr., famous authoress-philosopher Anäis Nin, and a group of Russian refugees along with a colony of well-to-do Filipino families. One of those Russian refugees was none other than Maria Rasputin, daughter of Imperial Russia's "mad monk" who'd been friend and advisor to Czarina Alexandra. He figured in Russia's plots and counter-plots prior to the Soviet Revolution, and acquired a huge following among Czarist Russia's nobility. At his assassination Maria fled to Paris, then to Los Angeles. Keeping her true identity hidden from most of her neighbors, she resided in a two-bedroom cottage on Larissa Street off Sunset. Just prior to her death in 1977 she authored a book defending the reputation of her famous father.

The Dust Bowl influx of the thirties added to the conglomeration of residents. Low-rent housing attracted them, and the flatlands below Sunset provided ideal soil for their backyard gardens. Many of them, though, settled in Echo Park to be near Sister Aimee. Their idol had "brought them to God" back on the Oklahoma plains or on the prairies of northern Texas. In Echo Park they found her well and happy, preaching to the multitudes in her cavernous temple every Sunday night.

In the dreary years of 1932 and 1933, when jobs were scarce and many families lacked money for even the simplest sustenance, Aimee opened her doors every weekend to lines of hungry people backing up all the way around Lemoyne Street to Sunset, and on down the Boulevard, awaiting her gifts of bread, meat, canned food, milk, and other staples. "We are the Lord's instrument," she told her church officials, "so these people *must* be fed, even if we starve ourselves...." And so, every Saturday, month after month, thousands queued up along the sidewalks of Sunset Boulevard to receive their gifts from the kind lady by the lake.

Since those miserable days, when many stores were shuttered and shelves were almost bare, Echo Park businesses have come and gone along Sunset Boulevard. A few have survived, though, and are still operating. Old, funky Pioneer Market has sat on Echo Park Avenue at Sunset for years. Lord's Jewelers, the Sunset Cocktail Bar, Stefan's Shoe Store and Shoe Repair, the Sunset Pharmacy, and Minette's Antiques also remain to serve their loyal patrons — some of whom drive down from the highest hills of Silver Lake.

Echo Park boasts some fine restaurants, too — one of them considered among the top ten in Los Angeles. Three of the most popular sit on Sunset, within one block of each other. The most famous is Les Freres Taix, serving mainly French provincial entrees. Established in 1927 near the Plaza, it moved westward to Echo Park in 1965 to make room for a new city-owned parking lot adjacent to the Civic Center. Barragan's Cafe is also excellent, and for superb Mexican dishes El Rodeo stands out among all those along the Boulevard. To satisfy the Boulevard's pastry *aficionados*, Celaya Bakery is located across the street from old Pioneer Market.

Down from the bakery, the mammoth Jensen's Recreation Center still stands. Old and worn, the huge brick building once served as a private health club, with overnight rooms above its main facilities available to members. Many famous athletes, including Joe Louis and Jackie Robinson, were invited to make personal appearances here in the later years just prior to the club's closing. Several years ago, to commemorate these appearances, an Echo Park improvement organization acquired funds and the approval of city officials to have attractive bronze plaques citing each of these sports figures placed into the sidewalks. Beginning at Laveta Terrace and going four blocks west to the Park Avenue turnoff, the distinctive plaques are imbedded along the north side of Sunset Boulevard.

As a recent Urban Studies Report put it, Echo Park is composed of a "remarkable socio-economic mixture." Yet this robust, culturally diverse community hums with ethnic varieties, including festivals, parades, decorated store fronts, and some eccentric citizens. It boasts rural pleasures, too, such as canoeing, picnics, and flower shows, as well as community projects, little theater groups, evening arts and crafts classes, and writers' clubs. Echo Park is spirited — still proud of its complex heritage and its imposing temple.

The Angelus Temple's current director is the Reverend Rolf McPherson. As Aimee's only son, he reigns over the International Church of the Foursquare Gospel, headquartered in a handsome high-rise building facing Sunset just a block away. He and his Church have established a large Bible school in the neighborhood, and many of its students occupy low-rent apartments along Sunset as well as Lemoyne Street, where Sister Aimee once resided with her mother and daughter.

America's Dream Street stretches twenty-seven miles from the Plaza to the sea, and the Echo Park section is probably the only segment considered seedy. The annual median income for the entire area, from lower Silver Lake east to Barragan's Cafe, is less than $6,800. Its architectural hodge-podge recently was likened by a Los Angeles journalist to multicolored pieces of marzipan on a platter of white mints, each piece decorated with graffiti — unsavory-looking, but having "interest" and "character". It's a special part of Sunset Boulevard that has remained un-cosmeticized. No impressive homes sparkle like gems — no tennis courts, no wide, divided thoroughfares, and not a single Rolls Royce. People romanticize Echo Park for its few remaining pastoral qualities, but realists usually exclaim — as did a recent visitor from Florida — "My God, how grim!"

Grim, shabby, artistic, sylvan, and eccentric, it *is* unique. The first suburb that developed out of the Plaza, it's the back door to Hollywood. The part of Sunset Boulevard dubbed un-glamorous, Echo Park is hospitable, friendly, simple, and definitely un-plastic — very unlike its neighbor to the west.

After tunnel cutting was completed, citizens from Los Angeles and the Echo Park district turned out to celebrate "Tunnel Day" in September of 1909, driving westward along Sunset Boulevard. Newspaper stories tell of lemonade stands set up to cater to passing motorists and passengers. [Title Insurance and Trust Company] □

Sunset Boulevard, looking east into downtown Echo Park. Jensen's Recreation Center and Apartments is in the center. □ Jensen's Recreation Center, a men's health club built around 1919, stands in the heart of Echo Park. Several famous athletes, including Gene Tunney, Joe Louis, and Jackie Robinson, have presented demonstrations to sports fans here. Headquarters of the Worldwide Church of the Foursquare Gospel, founded by Aimee Semple McPherson, are located in the California Federal Savings and Loan Building at right. □

Inlaid plaques honoring
famous athletes appear for
several blocks along Sunset
Boulevard sidewalks in Echo
Park. This district is a
melting pot for various ethnic
groups, primarily recent
immigrants from Cuba and other
Latin American countries. □

43

The impressive Angelus Temple conceived by Aimee Semple McPherson for the thousands who came to hear her preach. When Sister Aimee passed the plates for "offerings" she demanded — and got — "greenbacks, no loose change." □

A service at the Angelus Temple in 1935, with not one empty seat. Sister Aimee, in a white robe with her hand raised, preaches from in front of the choir. [Rev. Rolf McPherson] □

Baptism over the radio? Sister Aimee and an assistant minister baptize a married couple, with a microphone in foreground to carry her words over Los Angeles airwaves. Aimee Semple

McPherson passed away in 1944 and was buried on her 54th birthday. [Rev. Rolf McPherson] □

The #5138 streetcar bears left onto Sunset to merge into Hollywood Boulevard at Virgil, near the site of the old Biograph Studios in January, 1950. Part of the Angelus Temple is in the background at right. [Interurbans Publications] □

A Pacific Electric "red car" has just left Sunset Boulevard in the distance and glides down Park Avenue toward Glendale Boulevard in the foreground. These famous streetcars shuttled multitudes of worshipers to and from Aimee's church for Sunday evening services. Photo taken in 1951. [Interurbans Publications] □

In 1904 the dwelling at right sat almost where the Angelus Temple is now. The Sunset Boulevard bridge is in the distance. A group of Mexican and black children wave as horseless carriages pass along Glendale Boulevard. [Title Insurance and Trust Company] □

Members of the exclusive Los Angeles Automobile Club on an outing in the Echo Park district. Sunset Boulevard was not paved when this photo was taken in September, 1904, and motorists preferred the smoother driving surface of the sidewalk. [Title Insurance and Trust Company] □

Echo Park made history when
snow fell on January 11, 1949.
Harry Truman had just become
President and along with the
news of his inauguration, papers
and radios announced the first
"heavy" snowfall in 35 years.
[Michael J. Greene] □

Echo Park Lake in 1897, one year after its inception. The Sanford house is at right. [Authors' Collection] □
In 1911 Echo Park Lake was surrounded by spacious homes built by suburbanites wanting to get away from the hustle and bustle of the Plaza. Several of these dwellings remain, but today the lake is surrounded mostly by apartments and commercial structures. In the background is Mt. Hollywood. [Los Angeles Public Library] □

Today giant water lilies, palm
trees and the lake peacefully
coexist with nearby Civic Center
high rises. □

An early photo of Wyatt Earp, famed gunfighter, bad man and marshall. Earp retired to Los Angeles, lived for awhile on Sunset Boulevard near Alvarado Street, then moved to 17th Street near Crenshaw where he died in 1929. [Authors' Collection] □

This publicity photo of Tom Mix was probably taken at his Mixville Studios just north of Echo Park in the mid 1930s. A shopping center has since replaced the studios. [Authors' Collection] □

Poetess, authoress, diarist, Anäis Nin resided in Echo Park near Sunset Boulevard for many years. Her writings became famous for their erotic overtones and in the late 1970s saw a rebirth in popularity. [UCLA Collection] ☐

"Tourist" cabins which later became low- rent apartments are stacked up on this Sunset Boulevard lot. Wyatt Earp may have lived here while acting as a consultant on two Tom Mix movies. □

Known throughout the world as Tonto in the Lone Ranger movies, Jay Silverheels was very active in Indian affairs. He lived in Echo Park, where he conducted an acting school for Indians, prior to his death early in 1980. [Tom Shelly Enterprises] ☐

Sunset Boulevard cuts through a hill in Echo Park, near Coronado Street just west of Alvarado, in 1909. Some segments of Sunset's westward expansion required as many as 350 men and 250 teams of mules. Seven million cubic feet of dirt were required to fill one area between Douglas and Maltman Streets. *The Examiner* newspaper reported at the time, "Sunset Boulevard as it is today…is a splendid thoroughfare destined soon to become a most popular outlet into a beautiful suburban country . . . ." [Bruce Torrence Historical Collection, Pacific Federal Savings] ☐

The cut at Coronado in 1980, 71 years later. Upon completion of the cut Los Angeles citizens proclaimed, "…now the Boulevard gives us the most scenic route out of Los Angeles for automobile or horse and buggy…." ☐

Another hill bowing to Sunset Boulevard's progress, this one near Silver Lake Avenue in 1909. The surrounding "country" is now completely filled with residential, commercial and high-rise developments. [Bruce Torrence Historical Collection, Pacific Federal Savings] □ Below, Sanford Street curves off Sunset and wraps around the most prominent hill of Silver Lake, an area adjacent to Echo Park that was built around a man-made reservoir. □

In the top photo, the West Olive sub-station at Sunset and Silver Lake, around 1920. [Interurbans Publications] □

Now occupied by a group of architects, the West Olive sub-station has taken on pastel colors, a new roof and a garden. □

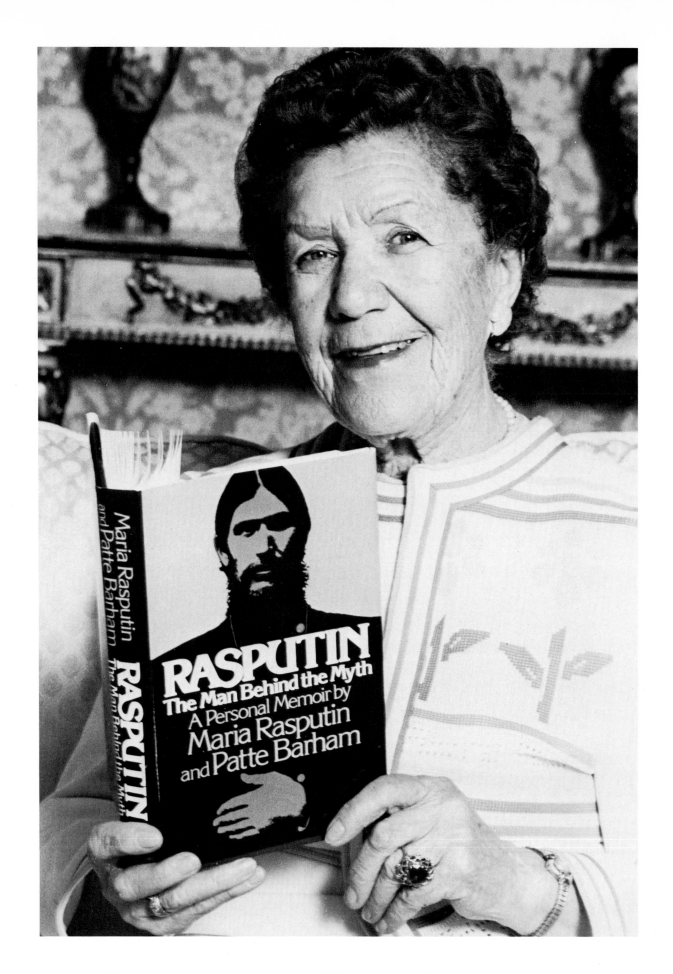

62

Maria Rasputin, daughter of Imperial Russia's "Mad Monk", resided in the Silver Lake-Echo Park section of Sunset Boulevard. After her father's death, Maria fled Russia and spent the remainder of her life defending his reputation. [Patte Barham Collection] □ Sunset Boulevard crosses over Silver Lake Avenue on a bridge recently declared an historical cultural monument by the City of Los Angeles. Romanesque arches support the 1934 bridge which lies just a few blocks east of the old Mabel Normand Studios. □

A merchant's street fair was held in 1980 to bring together and stabilize relations between various ethnic groups residing in the western part of Echo Park and Silver Lake. The fair featured ethnic foods and entertainment. □

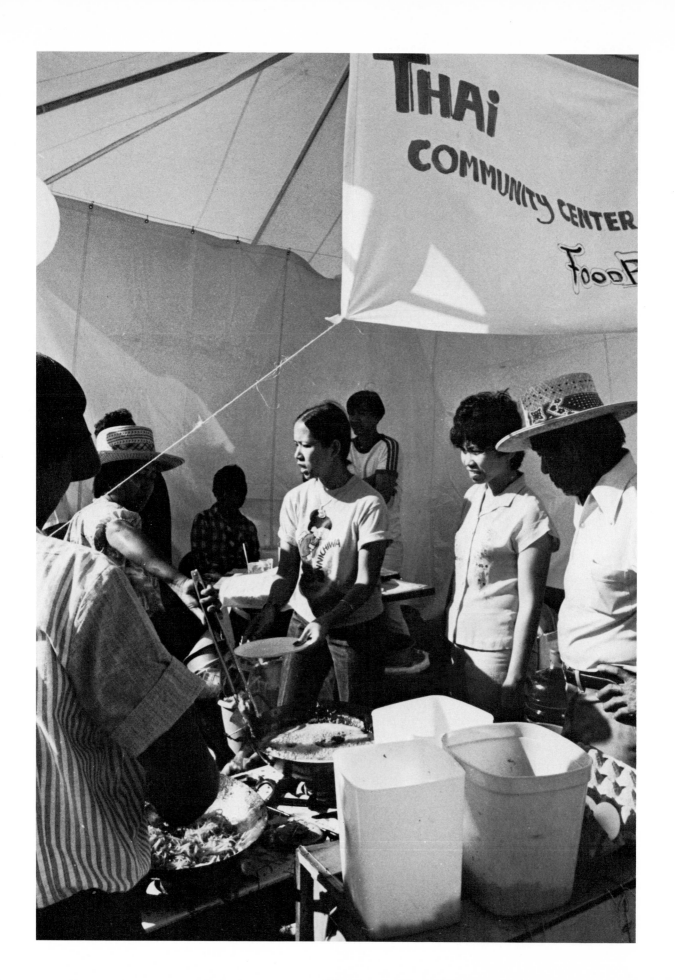

HOLLYWOOD
One-Reelers to Color T.V.

Sunset Boulevard was there — a muddy little path about thirty feet wide — when Horace Wilcox came out from the midwest and built a farmhouse about three miles west of Echo Park. He planted a small lemon orchard, set out a twenty-acre vineyard alongside cucumber patches, and grew prosperous from his produce. Three narrow roads, linked end-to-end, led eastward back to Echo Park from the Sunset Boulevard section, which lay directly below the farmhouse. As Echo Park's population expanded toward the Wilcox farm, the demand for land grew.

That was in the early 1870s. In 1877 Wilcox decided to subdivide his land and cash in on the real estate boom. He mapped out streets and lots, thoughtfully allocating areas for parks and picnic grounds. He created two roads leading north off Sunset and named them Wilcox and Weyse. A few years later Weyse was renamed Vine Street. Above Sunset Boulevard he laid out a parallel street and called it Prospect Avenue, which eventually became Hollywood Boulevard. Lots along Sunset and up Weyse Street sold so fast that customers waited in lines at Wilcox's office to make down payments. Jacob Stern, a German immigrant, bought one of the lots on Weyse about 400 feet north of Sunset and built a barn to shelter his cow and several goats. That barn made history — it was a signal landmark of the motion picture industry.

Wilcox probably was so happy raking in money from his property sales that he couldn't possibly have contemplated the accelerated growth that would not only devour his modest estate but everything around it. How could he or his wife of twenty-seven years ever have imagined that within sixteen years the little town she had named Hollywood would grow to nearly 3,000 inhabitants living in 900 homes! And how could they have imagined that within a few more years Sunset Boulevard would be a heavily traveled thoroughfare

carrying people to and from work at the moving picture factories, that scores of millionaires would be created from an industry that prints tiny "moving" pictures on thin strips of celluloid, that their peaceful little Hollywood would gain notoriety throughout the world, and that their own backyard garden would become part of a popular tourist attraction known as the Hollywood Hotel? Yet it happened. Sunset Boulevard became that famous artery which moved the vital flow of industry and tourism. Today — even though Horace Wilcox could never have dreamed such a dream — it moves bumper-to-bumper.

The small orchards were still there. Fragrant rose gardens and hibiscus bushes lined the narrower roads, small cactus gardens still grew in front yards, a few short streets boasted borders of palm trees imported from Hawaii and brought in from San Diego, and a few pebble-strewn roads hugged the lower slopes of the hills, trailing leisurely alongside small orange groves toward Cahuenga Pass. But Wilcox's thriving little community soon became a make-believe world. Eager bands of men appeared, hand-cranking their peculiar cameras. From Chicago and New York they came with satchels full of money — and Sunset Boulevard would feel their Midas touch for decades to come.

It happened quickly and quietly. On a crisp November day in 1907 Francis Boggs and Thomas Persons stepped off the train in Los Angeles and took a ride out Sunset. These two men founded Hollywood's motion picture industry. They had begun a one-reel version of *The Count of Monte Cristo* in Chicago, but lacked adequate light for their sets. Artificial studio lighting had not yet been invented. Indoor scenes were shot against three decorated partitions under an open-air ceiling and on cold days cameras would catch the actors breathing steam from their mouths. So when the pair caught word of the marvelous year-round warmth and sun out in Southern California, they quickly packed their bulky equipment and headed west. Boggs and Persons originally set up their offices near Fourth Street a short distance from the Plaza in Los Angeles. Then they moved to Echo Park for a few months, and from there to Hollywood. They housed their equipment and supplies at what is now 6050 Sunset Boulevard, later to become the short-lived Christie Studios. They made no notable movies, however, and Hollywood's memory has long since buried them.

Not forgotten, though, are such legendary moguls as William Fox, founder of giant Twentieth Century-Fox; Louis B. Mayer, a former junk dealer; Jesse L. Lasky; Samuel Goldwyn; Joseph Schenck; Jack Warner; Adolph Zukor, who just recently died at the age of 103; Barney Balaban; Mack Sennett; Spyros Skouras; Cecil B. DeMille; and others, including such famous director-geniuses as Erich Von Stroheim, Fritz Lang, Victor Fleming, and the great D. W. Griffith. And what old veteran of Hollywood pictures can forget the master cameraman of them all, Billy Bitzer, who lived briefly in a small apartment on Sunset near Gordon Street while filming Griffith's *Broken Blossoms* and *Intolerance*? (In his book on filming D. W. Griffith's movies, Bitzer tells of Griffith sending a young man down Sunset to Mom's Lunch Room near Vermont Avenue to order 950 sandwiches "to go" for the cast and technicians on the *Intolerance* set who hadn't found time to break for lunch.) These were magical names whose owners left lasting impressions on Hollywood and all around the globe — and, of course, each of them traversed time and again over the dirt, asphalt, and cement pavement of Sunset Boulevard.

Most of Hollywood's movie studios were constructed on Sunset. At the junction with Hollywood Boulevard, where Sunset veers to the left going west, the Mutual Studios were erected. Kinemacolor Studios, the small company that conducted experiments in color photography as early as 1913, lay next door. It was on these lots that *Intolerance* was filmed; Griffith had leased them and renamed the studios Griffith-Fine Arts. *Intolerance*'s magnificent set of the Babylonian palace of King Belshazzar — a mammoth structure that took months to build — stood directly across the street on the north side of Sunset and stretched over a quarter-mile down the Boulevard. Hollywood oldtimers remember crowds gathered on Sunset to watch the filming, in which more than 2,500 players and extras scaled the huge edifice,

engaged in hand-to-hand combat, and even rode chariots over the parapets 175 feet above the ground — without nets. Griffith-Fine Arts Studios also gave the world *Birth of a Nation*, another masterpiece produced and directed by Griffith. Today a modern shopping center and paved parking lots serving a nearby hospital occupy the sprawling grounds.

Typically American, Hollywood is known for its compassion and generosity. With help from neighboring communities, it has conducted several lavish fund-raising drives and built the ultra-modern Children's Hospital. It's the largest medical facility of its kind in America, rising majestically on the southeast corner of Sunset and Vermont Avenue. Recently its clinics and additional wings have been underwritten by grants from a wealthy Los Angeles couple who've already poured thirty million dollars into the building fund. Many film and television celebrities, though, still help support the hospital with their large annual contributions.

Intolerance was made in 1917, but another classic — often referred to as Hollywood's "pioneer" film — preceded *Intolerance* by four years. In December of 1913 Jesse L. Lasky, Cecil B. DeMille and Samuel Goldwyn rented Jake Stern's little barn on Weyse Street off Sunset, set up their cameras and started rolling. The first full-length movie made in Hollywood, *The Squaw Man*, was soon released. Some controversy has arisen out of the scanty records kept in those days. Some say the film was actually made in and around that barn, and a plaque commemorating the event now appears at the entrance to the American Savings and Loan building there. But down the street, on the famous corner of Sunset and Vine, a larger plaque was set into the sidewalk in 1954 in front of the Home Savings and Loan building claiming that *The Squaw Man* was made *there*. Perhaps the film's scenes were shot over the entire span of that large lot, from the barn down to the corner itself, which would make *both* plaques accurate!

Soon after *The Squaw Man* was released, Lasky, together with Joseph Schenck and a group of actor-investors called the Famous Players built a tar-papered warehouse on the former site of Home Savings and Loan. Known as the Lasky Studio, it cranked out numerous shorts and features — and made Lasky a fortune. He later teamed up with Charlie Chaplin, D. W. Griffith, Douglas Fairbanks, and Mary Pickford to form United Artists, the largest film distributing company in the world.

Inside the savings and loan building vivid murals, designed and painted under the supervision of artist Millard Sheets, feature scenes from *The Squaw Man*, commemorating filmdom's beginning. The entrance to the edifice glows with a myriad of color from a fabulous stained-glass window designed by Susan Hertel. Capturing the drama of Hollywood's film industry, the window gives colorful glimpses of the Keystone Cops, Harold Lloyd's *Safety Last*, Buster Keaton, cowboys and Indians, gangster chases, *The Phantom of the Opera*, *Moby Dick* and the Marx Brothers — a collage of history and color!

In 1954 the Hollywood Chamber of Commerce buried a time capsule below the sidewalk, directly under the large *Squaw Man* plaque. To be dug up in the year 2004, the capsule — a lucite box within a steel box — contains, among other items, photographs of the ceremony, a golden record of Bing Crosby singing "White Christmas," a television episode of "I Love Lucy," a 1954 radio tape of "The Jack Benny Show," Golden-Year special editions of Hollywood trade journals and the script of *Gone With The Wind*. The marker dubs Sunset and Vine "the most famous corner in the world" — the plaque, the murals and the stained glass window attract thousands of tourists to the corner every year.

After Lasky, old William Fox came to town. Fox had made — and lost — two enormous fortunes in the movies, camera patents, and theater operations businesses, one fortune reaching $300 million around 1925. Some of the great stars to shine from the Fox Studios were Tom Mix, Theda Bara, Elissa Landi, Will Rogers, Shirley Temple, and Janet Gaynor. Fox bought twenty acres on the southwest and southeast corners of Sunset at Western Avenue to build his Twentieth Century-Fox Studios. For seven years he'd headed up his own Fox Film Corporation in New York, but eventually merged with a group of New York investors including Harley Clarke, Ed Tucker and Adolph Zukor, mainly because he needed their hard cash to pull him from the depths of bankruptcy. Fox ended up in jail for stock manipulation, but his studios have survived through the present. The original structures, though, were recently demolished and the land leased to a major shopping center. Most of the company and its West Coast office moved to West Los Angeles and now owns the entire leased acreage on which sits the ultra-modern steel-and-glass, high-rise portion of Los Angeles called Century City.

After Griffith's Babylon set was torn down in the early twenties, a company called Monogram occupied studios on the same spot facing Sunset. That corporation turned out hundreds of low-budget films known as the "B-pictures" — westerns, comedies, mysteries, short novelty features, and sob-sister melodramas. Part of the *Three Stooges* series was made there, as well as the first *Dracula* pictures and many others now resting in "crypts" on the back shelves of Hollywood's extensive archives. The Monogram buildings were later converted for use by a company called Vitagraph Studios. Today the once-again remodeled studios house KCET, an up-to-date educational television station producing some of the finest public service programs in America.

Barely half a mile farther west on Sunset Columbia Pictures set up shop on a twelve-acre lot at Gower, where the Nestor Studio was built nearly two years before. Columbia produced top-quality dramas there, as well as better mysteries and westerns. Over the years the corner of Sunset and Gower became known as "Gower Gulch", as movie extras with grubby checkered shirts, boots, holsters, and unshaven faces beneath crumpled cowboy hats, hung around in small clusters awaiting calls from the casting office for $10-a-day walk-on (or ride-on) parts. In the block shared with Columbia's sound stages a man named Jerry Fairbanks became famous producing innumerable short subjects which showed in theaters along with feature films. Sunset and Gower, however, also saw some losers. A whole slew of movie studios came and went over a brief eight-year span. On the Columbia lot cameras still whir today, albeit electronically. The big lot across the street from Columbia's entrance has been converted to yet another shopping complex — appropriately, it's called "Gower Gulch Shopping Center." The only thing that has disappeared from the Columbia complex itself is the Pathé Brothers Hollywood office, housed there in the twenties to direct the Paris firm's world-wide newsreel episodes.

After operating their nickelodeon "arcade" in New York for a couple of years the four Warner brothers appeared on the Hollywood scene and built studios on Sunset, barely three blocks from Gower Gulch. They designed a handsome general office building facing the Boulevard with an impressive facade of Roman columns spanning its front. Behind it they built five sound stages. The office structure is considered one of the most striking buildings in downtown Hollywood today, having been well maintained and refurbished over the past five decades. Radio station KMPC and television station KTLA, both owned by Gene Autry's Golden West Broadcasting Company, now occupy the premises.

Farther westward, on the southeast corner of Sunset and La Brea Avenue, Charlie Chaplin built his Chaplin Studios. Resembling a tiny Tyrolean village, the studios sat on six acres directly behind his second home. Most of the great Chaplin films were made on this compact lot, and occasionally Chaplin would lease out the stages to independent producers. An ugly supermarket has replaced Chaplin's home, but the studios are still there, repainted and refurbished. The master comedian, a resident of Switzerland during his last twenty years, paid a nostalgic call at the studios during his much-publicized visit to Hollywood in 1972, walking quietly near the front section of the small lot while admirers watched silently at the sidelines. Imagine the fading flashbacks, the cherished memories, which must have flickered through the old man's brilliant mind during those brief moments!

Studios came and went along Sunset Boulevard. Only the "biggies", the "giants", survived and are operating today, many of them having turned to profitable television series production. Except for Metro-Goldwyn-Mayer, RKO, Paramount, and Universal, they all were on, or within a few hundred feet of, Sunset Boulevard. Collectively they employed thousands of people. Actors, technicians, writers, directors, artists, tradesmen, accountants, costume designers, seamstresses, and many others dedicated themselves to the manufacture of dreams and fantasies designed to lull America's — and the world's — audiences away from real life. Maybe a small segment of those dreams and fantasies were vicariously fulfilled in the lives of Hollywood's visitors through the glamorous night life they found in entertainment "palaces" and intimate night clubs along the Boulevard. These fantasies were lived, too, by Hollywood's own citizens, seeking respite from hard work at the dream factories or their day-to-day lives.

The Boulevard has always sported fine restaurants and night clubs. Several — repeatedly mentioned in fan magazines, newspaper columns and radio shows — became household words. "The most beautiful girls in the world" passed through the portals of Earl Carroll's; across the street was The Hollywood Palladium. A block off Sunset The Brown Derby sat adjacent to the former sight of the old *Squaw Man* barn, and

Musso and Frank's, one of the earliest restaurants to open in Hollywood, is just two blocks off Sunset.

Night after night, year after year, enthusiastic crowds gathered up the street from Gower Gulch at the spacious Palladium to be entertained by such greats as Jimmy Dorsey and His Band, Benny Goodman, Harry James, Tony Bennett, Ginny Simms, Frank Sinatra, Margaret Whiting, the Andrews Sisters, Tony Martin, Spike Jones, the Mills Brothers, Alice Faye, Frankie Laine, and countless others. For several years many of the popular "Queen For a Day" radio shows were broadcast from Earl Carroll's in the morning, while evening entertainment consisted of songs and dances by some of America's most beautiful show girls, spotlighted in glittering costumes and feather-trimmed gowns that only a Hollywood designer could create. Several of Carroll's showgirls hit the movies, including Sheree North, Jean Wallace, Marie MacDonald, and others. On the exterior walls dozens of gigantic celebrity autographs were inscribed, sidewalk to roof, across huge protruding square blocks covering the entire front wall. Motorists faithfully congested traffic as they slowed to gawk at those magical names! Up the street, on Vine, expectant crowds gathered daily outside the main entrance of The Brown Derby in hopes of seeing stars drop in for lunch or cocktails. A "regular" was Jimmy Durante. Three or four times a week, for many years, he could be seen entering with his closest friends for cocktails and dinner.

The Palladium is still there. Built in 1940 by *Los Angeles Times* owner Norman Chandler, its ground-breaking was performed by Lana Turner, who used a silver-plated shovel for the ceremony. It has been slightly remodeled since, and more recently has been made famous by Lawrence Welk's weekly television broadcasts, several T.V. Emmy Award programs, and rock music concerts. Also, numerous private organizations rent the hall for their annual banquets and dances. Marriott Corporation, the emporium's present owner, estimates that more than thirty-nine million people have attended Palladium events. Earl Carroll's has changed hands six times over the past twenty-six years, serving as small theatres in three instances. It was called the Aquarius Theatre when the Broadway hit musical *Hair* opened there in the mid 1960s. It has been four other theatres since, including a stint as the Long Horn Theater. Now, once again, it's the Aquarius. The Brown Derby still operates, but the stars — and with them, the eager clusters of autograph seekers — have disappeared. It now serves a clientele of tourists and local merchants.

In 1927 the Schwab brothers opened a tiny drugstore on Sunset near the beginning of the Strip. Much has been written about the stars who supposedly were "discovered" behind its counters and soda fountain. Actually, nobody who has reveled in Hollywood's limelight was discovered while working at Schwab's, but the patrons who've dropped in for a cup of coffee or a malted have probably turned it into the most famous drugstore in America.

Schwab's is only three blocks west of Fairfax Avenue. Just one block farther, on the same side of the Boulevard, is an attractive Savings and Loan complex surrounded by neatly terraced flower beds and patios. On these same grounds in the mid-twenties actress Alla Nazimova built her fabulous *Garden of Allah*, a village of apartments and bungalows shining brightly in the California sun. Its graceful Spanish architecture eliciting "oohs" and "ahs" from passing motorists, it was home to F. Scott Fitzgerald, Charles Butterworth, Christopher Isherwood, Rudolph Valentino, Constance Talmadge, Edna Mae Oliver, Donald Crisp, Linda Darnell, Robert Benchley, Peter Lorre, Errol Flynn, violinist Mischa Elman, Madame Schumann-Heink, Rachmaninoff, and dozens of others. The magnificent Garden disappeared in 1965, when it fell prey to the demolition ball.

As the radio and motion picture studios grew, so did Hollywood. Its population expanded and small businesses mushroomed, particularly along Sunset. Automobile traffic tripled between 1932 and 1940, and Hollywood High School's enrollment doubled. (Among its graduates: Dwayne Hickman, Lana Turner, Natalie Wood, Carol Burnett, and Jerry "Beaver" Mathers.) Drive-in eating places popped up on major corners and a new word was coined — the "car-hop", a shapely young waitress or fresh-faced young man who served meals on a tray at your car window. The Carpenter's Drive-Ins, one of which was on the northwest corner of Sunset and La Brea, were undoubtedly the best known.

With the boom in entertainment came a boom in jobs. The thriving motion picture studios were magnets around which smaller firms sprang up — there was hardly a company, large or small, that wasn't a satellite to a studio or one of its affiliates.

The two entertainment giants, Columbia Broadcasting System and National Broadcasting Company, hired hundreds of audio specialists and support personnel at the height of their success. For three decades their profits shot sky-high as businesses eagerly paid enormous sums to sponsor such shows as "Amos 'n' Andy," the "Fred Allen Show," "Fibber McGee and Molly," "Lum 'n' Abner," "Jack Benny," the "Gracie Allen Show," "Sam Spade," "Kate Smith," "The Shadow," "Inner Sanctum," and "Lux Radio Theater."

Where were those famous studios built? On Sunset Boulevard, of course, right in the heart of Hollywood! CBS was built, and remodeled fifteen years later, on the northwest corner of Gower Gulch. The facilities are still in use today, some of the smaller auditoriums having been transformed into television production stages. The studio also contains the offices of Columbia Records. NBC has come and gone on Sunset Boulevard, having relocated in nearby Burbank in 1964, but the studios once stood on none other than the "most famous corner in the world" — Sunset and Vine — on the very sight of Lasky's studio, the *Squaw Man* plaque, and the time capsule. For years the pale blue NBC buildings were a Hollywood landmark, and tourists mailed countless thousands of post cards bearing their image throughout the world. It was a sad day when the structures were torn down in 1966.

A few blocks farther west, just before Hollywood High School at Highland Avenue, there is a collection of small cottages, each quite unlike another, surrounding small "plazas". This tight little group of buildings, spreading from the sidewalk on the north side of Sunset back to a narrow, parallel street named Selma, is called "Crossroads of the World." Although some of them have been remodeled, these bungalows are among the oldest in downtown Hollywood. Built originally as low-rent apartments, they eventually evolved into tiny offices, some with an upper story in Tudor style protruding over the Spanish plazas and flower beds below. The famous California artist Buckley MacGurrin lived there in 1925 and 1926, and "Alfalfa" Switzer of the "Our Gang" comedies resided there with his parents in the early thirties. The largest cottage facing Sunset is now occupied by a casting office.

Almost next door is the beautiful Church of the Blessed Sacrament, where many of filmdom's great attend mass. Not far from the church, on the same side of the Boulevard, stood Wallich's Music City, for four decades one of Hollywood's pioneer music publishing companies and musical instrument retailers. On a dare from a friend, one of the three Wallich brothers founded another Hollywood landmark, the gigantic Capitol Records company. Housed in a distinctive thirteen-story round building north of Sunset near Vine, it appears in just about any view of the city. Across from the Sacrament church stands a graceful two-story office building owned for many years by Edgar Bergen. Two of its most famous tenants are the national Caroline Leonetti Charm School offices and the Mou-Ling Restaurant. Bergen bought the property for $150,000 and sold it before his recent death for $1,200,000. Practically next door the famous movie make-up geniuses, the Westmore brothers, ran their studio. And just a short walk from the Bergen building stood the New England-style studio of Max Munn Autry, the man who probably photographed more Hollywood celebrities than any other portrait photographer in the world. His studio is now a real estate office.

Right there, in the middle of all these landmarks that made Hollywood great, stood the Canteen — legendary despite its brief existence. At the outbreak of World War II thousands of soldiers, marines and sailors streamed into Hollywood on weekend passes. Restaurants, bars and theatres bulged to the brim. Servicemen walked the streets and hung around corners in search of ways to fill their short visits to the magic city. They had read all the fan magazines and seen all the movies, and now they wanted to see *real* movie stars, so they headed for the Hollywood Canteen. The Canteen was the brainchild of a handful of patriotic Hollywood citizens who wanted to pay tribute to our men and women at war. Among them were Bette Davis and Jane Russell. With other civic leaders and a group of Hollywood merchants, they called upon fellow motion picture celebrities to come forward and help — the response was overwhelming.

In an old building on Cahuenga, just 150 feet south of Sunset, this legend consisted of a small stage, a dance floor, and facilities for serving food and non-alcoholic refreshments. Volunteers showed up by the dozens to clean, repaint, polish woodwork, and make minor repairs to the aging structure. The Hollywood Canteen was born almost overnight. Within a few weeks word spread from San Diego to Houston: movie stars were playing host to servicemen! With press and radio

news coverage the Canteen soon claimed national attention. Every week men and women on leave swarmed into Hollywood by the thousands to rub elbows with the stars. Betty Grable is said to have stunned a sergeant one Saturday night by grabbing his hand and insisting he jitterbug with her. A marine was delighted one night when Olivia de Havilland offered to sew on a button which had dropped off his jacket. Stars appeared in shifts, entertaining the servicemen each night from about seven o'clock till midnight. When they weren't entertaining or dancing they served refreshments and washed dishes.

During its four-year life the Canteen saw some grand evenings — Eddie Cantor entertained; Danny Kaye performed by the hour; the Andrews Sisters sang "In Apple Blossom Time;" Judy Garland danced til her feet ached; Ida Lupino gave impressions of London music hall girls; Marie Wilson and Ken Murray presented skits from their hit show, *Blackouts*; and Edgar Bergen matched wits with Charlie McCarthy and Mortimer Snerd to the howls of appreciative GIs. Others who made regular appearances at the Canteen — when they happened to be in town or had an evening to spare — were Helen Hayes, Victor Mature, Victor Borge, Hans Conreid, Danny Thomas, Red Skelton, Cesar Romero, Van Johnson, Keenan Wynn, Hedy LaMarr, Martha Raye, Howard Duff, Dorothy Lamour, Mickey Rooney, Anita Luise, Donna Reed, Elsa Lanchester, Dinah Shore — the list is endless. What delighted the patrons most was the standing rule that the Canteen was off-limits to brass. Commissioned officers had their own plush clubs in the Los Angeles area from which enlisted men were excluded — the Canteen was exclusively rank-and-file.

How did all these members of the armed forces reach the exalted night spot? From downtown Los Angeles, buses and trains disgorged them like coins from a slot machine, and Sunset Boulevard carried them to Hollywood. Most of them disembarked at Union Station, where Sunset Boulevard originated at the Plaza. There, rising from the area where Chinatown had sat for seventy-five years, Union Station became the hub of a giant railway complex which served the thousands of rail passengers who came in and out of Los Angeles every week. After twenty years of controversy, intrigue, and shuffling of bureaucratic papers, Los Angeles removed all traces of the original Chinatown by 1937. Ugly hovels and shacks were razed from the earth's surface. Below street level, surprised workers dug up crumbling cellars and dungeons, secret meeting rooms, and tunnels and catacombs, some zig-zagging beneath Sunset Boulevard. After much bickering and compromise among three railway companies, the Civic Center Association, the Municipal League, the Central Development Association, and Chinese elders who demanded a suitable relocation of their people's apartments, restaurants and stores, beautiful Union Station finally held its grand opening in May of 1939. More than 10,000 invited guests showed up for the grand affair. Newsreel cameramen caught all the excitement of celebrity appearances, VIP speeches, and band concerts as guests swarmed over the landscaped 200-car parking lot.

Union Station contains 78,000 square feet of floor space; its threshold is at the foot of Sunset Boulevard and extends 850 feet along Alameda Street. Visitors to the station are overwhelmed by its grand vestibule enhanced with Belgian black marble wainscot, travertine-bordered walls, and high, arched ceiling supported by massive black walnut beams. This majestic building helped make Sunset into a memorable boulevard. It came into being years after the historical motion picture studios were created and it lacked the romance of those film factories, but it did have its own glamour. From Union Station the GIs made their way to the Canteen. They knew that in that friendly old building near the corner of Cahuenga and Sunset a party would be going on — a party with dancing, music, entertainment, famous movie stars, and relief from the burden of war. And if that wasn't enough, they could hop a bus or hitchhike out beyond Schwab's, where a two-mile stretch of Sunset beckoned with nightclubs, fancy stores, gift shops, restaurants, drive-ins, and movie stars out for a late-night stroll. From downtown Hollywood everyone made a beeline for the Sunset Strip.

The remaining section of the old Mabel Normand Studios, built for the silent screen star by Mack Sennett. Normand produced one of her own pictures here, one block off Sunset at Fountain Avenue. The studio has been kept in excellent repair and is now occupied by Triangle Scenery Drapery and Lighting Company. ☐

The Mabel Normand Studios as they appeared in 1916. [Marc Wanamaker-Bison Archives] ☐

Mabel Normand at work in her studio, below. [Academy of Motion Picture Arts and Sciences] ☐

Mabel Normand in 1917.
[Academy of Motion Picture Arts
and Sciences] ☐
A Sunset Boulevard streetcar
approaches the Fountain Avenue
intersection in the early 1950s.
The Keystone Cleaners building
has recently been demolished.
[Interurbans Publications] ☐

Public Television Station KCET
occupies the remodeled
headquarters of the old
Monogram Studios, which
previously had been the Kalem
Studios. Other film companies
also used the building. ☐

A long-hidden projection
room, discovered behind a fake
wall was revealed at KCET in
1979 by two workmen who were
clearing rubble from an old
storage room. When facades
were torn away the room
revealed beautiful brickwork and
expert filigree, apparently
concealed by carpenters years
ago when Allied Artists occupied
the building. A guided tour is
conducted here by a KCET
official. □

The Monogram Studios, which produced the Dracula pictures and other B-rated films, at Sunset and Hoover in 1940. Much of the brick structure shown here at the rear of the building is still standing and being used today. Several production companies, including Allied Artists Corporation have used the facilities over the past five decades. [Marc Wanamaker-Bison Archives] □
Below, a western movie in progress at the Monogram Studios. [Marc Wanamaker-Bison Archives] □

Iron Eyes Cody, famous Hollywood film Indian, chats with Russell Ruiz, a descendant of one of Hollywood's original ranch families. This photo was taken at the studio of Public Television station KCET, originally the Kalem Company studio. The original northwest corner of Los Angeles' city limits, as first laid out by its founders, lies just a few feet from this spot. □

The old Biograph Studios spread over a huge lot at 4500 Sunset Boulevard, once the busiest movie producing corner in Hollywood, in 1916. Biograph became Triangle Pictures and changed names twice more before it was finally demolished.

Some of Hollywood's most famed silents were filmed here. At lower right a Hollywood Boulevard streetcar passes a small gas station, a portion of which stands today. [Marc Wanamaker-Bison Archives] □

The site of the Biograph Studios is now a parking lot for a supermarket, out of the picture at the left. At the right is part of Children's Hospital and at the lower right is the corner where the little gas station was seen in the previous photo. □

The main entrance to Children's Hospital of Los Angeles, next door to the site of the Biograph Studios where D.W. Griffith made his headquarters. The hospital is aided by generous donations of monied people in the television and movie industries. One family alone has given more than $30 million towards improvement and expansion of the hospital. □

The magnificent set of D.W. Griffith's *Intolerance* which stood on Sunset Boulevard from 1916 until the remaining portion was finally demolished in 1920. Famous movie photographer Billy Bitzer was chief cameraman for Griffith and wrote a fascinating account of filming this epic. [Bruce Torrence Historical Collection, Pacific Federal Savings] □

A rear view of the *Intolerance* set photographed in 1917 by Karl Brown from the roof of a residence at the corner of Talmadge and Prospect Avenues. Brown served on the famous movie's film crew as an assistant cameraman at the age of 18. Two of the houses in the foreground still stand. [Bruce Torrence Historical Collection, Pacific Federal Savings] □

Built on the site of the *Intolerance* set, Lou Bard's Hollywood Theatre held its grand opening on October 9, 1923. Featuring Baby Peggy in *Tips* and a personal appearance by the child star, Bard's Hollywood ushered in several Egyptian-style neighborhood theaters, some of which still operate. [Vista Theatre Collection] □

Operating today as the Vista
Theatre, much of the original
Egyptian motif remains. □

Triangle Pictures' Dorothy Gish
in a silent scene in 1917, filmed
at the Biograph Studios at 4500
Sunset Boulevard. [Marc
Wanamaker-Bison Archives] □

A stage crowded with actors and crew at Triangle Pictures in 1916. In front center are Douglas Fairbanks, Sr., Bessie Love, and director Allan Dwan. Others are bit players and extras. The man on the extreme left is believed to be Francis X. Bushman before he achieved stardom. [Marc Wanamaker-Bison Archives] □

Architect Frank Lloyd Wright designed this Aztec-inspired house for oil heiress Aline Barnsdall on Olive Hill at Sunset and Vermont. She named it the "Hollyhock House" and in 1927 gave the home and its eleven-acre grounds to the City of Los Angeles. Named Barnsdall Park, the area is used primarily for art classes and exhibits and cultural events. □

Below, the interior court of the house, former home of Aline Barnsdall. □

Looking west into downtown
Hollywood from Sunset Drive.
Unfortunately, the lovely hills in
the background are frequently
shrouded in smog. □

This scene was photographed around 1906 from the north edge of Sunset Boulevard showing Western Avenue — now a major Los Angeles thoroughfare — leading into the Los Feliz Hills. The famous Griffith Observatory now stands on the mound behind the large house. [Title Insurance and Trust Company] □

Below, Sunset and Western, looking north on Western towards Hollywood Boulevard. The children in the preceding photo were standing about 100 yards beyond the traffic signal shown here. □

The William Fox Studio just below Sunset on the west side of Western Avenue in 1937. The facilities sprawled over to the east side and took up nearly two full blocks. The company later became Twentieth Century Fox, then moved to west Los Angeles in an area that is now the fashionable Century City office complex. [Marc Wanamaker-Bison Archives] □

Below, a scene being filmed on the set of *Cleopatra*, starring Theda Bara, in 1917. The set covered a large corner of the William Fox Studio at Sunset and Western, and parts of it remained in use for the next year as sets for two more movies with historical themes. [Bruce Torrence Historical Collection, Pacific Federal Savings] □

Theda Bara, her husband, and
Norma Talmadge are greeted in
Los Angeles by Sid Grauman,
right, who leased Grauman's
Chinese Theatre from Hollywood
pioneer C. E. Toberman and
made the movie house a world
landmark with its "stars'
footprints in cement" in the
courtyard. [Authors' Collection]
□

The huge William Fox Studios along palm-lined Sunset Boulevard straddle both sides of Western Avenue in 1938. Two giant shopping centers occupy the grounds today. [Marc Wana-maker-Bison Archives] □ While tending her melon stand on Sunset between Western and Van Ness Avenues a farm woman pauses to be photographed in 1896. William Fox later produced some of Hollywood's greatest motion pictures on this site. [Security Pacific National Bank Historical Collections] □

The original West Coast studio
of the Warner Brothers sits in a
field of wild mustard in 1920.
Today the site, on Sunset
Boulevard near Van Ness, is
occupied by the Greek-columned
structure of radio station KMPC.

[Marc Wanamaker-Bison
Archives] □

Sunset Boulevard looking west from Van Ness Avenue in 1930. At left in the main building of the remodeled Warner Brothers Studio is radio station KFWB. The Hotel Eldorado across the street was for a short time the residence of noted director D.W. Griffith. Just two blocks down the Boulevard is the famed "Gower Gulch." [Security Pacific National Bank Historical Collections] ☐ The Warner Brothers location now houses television's KTLA Channel 5 and radio station KMPC, owned by former cowboy star Gene Autry. The Hotel Eldorado has become the St. Moritz and the trees, of course, have grown. ☐

The Warner Brothers and their studio, still standing, as it appeared in 1924. The brothers operated a chain of nickelodeons before going into movie production. They first started at the corner of Talmadge and Prospect Avenues where the ABC television studios are today. [Bruce Torrence Historical Collection, Pacific Federal Savings] □

Below, a western being filmed on the Sunset Boulevard lot of the Warner Brothers in 1924. [Marc Wanamaker-Bison Archives] □

VJ's cocktail bar on Sunset at Bronson was Cansino's Dance Studio before the stone front was installed. For ten years Cansino coached Hollywood stars and hopefuls. His own daughter, Rita, studied diligently and broke into show business as Rita Hayworth. ☐

The heavily traveled Sunset Boulevard offramp loops uphill to the right as Sunset crosses the Hollywood Freeway. The next ramp sign, barely visible over the Ventura sign, prepares motorists for Gower Street, whose intersection with Sunset has been dubbed "Gower Gulch" for the crowds of movie extras who hung around in western garb. In the background are the lovely Hollywood Hills. □

Gene Autry, who began his career as a singing cowboy, has become one of Hollywood's millionaires. He owns Golden West Broadcasting Company as well as other businesses and is very active in Hollywood civic affairs. 1980 marked Autry's 50th year in show business. [Golden West Broadcasting Company] □

Two Hollywood youngsters pose in the middle of Sunset just east of Gower Street at the turn of the century. Near the clump of trees at the right is the location of the original Columbia Studios buildings. [Title Insurance and Trust Company] □

Now the shade trees are gone and the Sunset-Gower Studios occupy buildings once owned by Columbia Studios. The "Columbia" building on the corner is a drug store and coffee shop. Are the little girls in the previous picture still with us, or are they gone also? □

The Columbia Studios on Gower Street in 1939. A sailor on the sidewalk eyes a billboard advertising *He Stayed for Breakfast*, starring Loretta Young and Melvyn Douglas. [Marc Wanamaker-Bison Archives] □

Below, a scene from Columbia's *Holiday*, filmed in 1939. [Columbia Pictures] □

On this spot many years ago movie "extras" gathered and waited for that lucky call from Columbia's casting office. The extras were already dressed in hats, chaps, and bandanas, prepared to be part of a crowd in a saloon, a member of a posse, or a ranch hand in the westerns that Columbia churned out about every ten days. Pay was usually $5 per day, $10 for a speaking part. □

The Cahuenga House in 1890, a store and restaurant owned by Mr. and Mrs. Blondeau, who sold meals, lager and liquor. It stood on the northwest corner of Sunset and Gower until the movie boom displaced it in 1915. The CBS offices occupy the site now. In the 1870s and '80s this area was called Cahuenga Valley until Mrs. Daeida Wilcox renamed it Hollywood. [Bruce Torrence Historical Collection, Pacific Federal Savings] □

The CBS building on Sunset and Gower, built in the late 1940s on the old Nestor Studios site. Although used primarily for offices now, the original building housed early radio stations. The company's major production facilities are at Beverly and Fairfax in West Hollywood. □

George Burns and Gracie
Allen on a CBS "Blue Network"
show, with guest Major Frank
Collins, in a 1939 broadcast. The
Blue Network was one of three
authorized by the U.S.

Government, but the term was
discarded when major companies
merged and acquired other
networks such as the Mutual Don
Lee Broadcasting Company.
[National Archives] □

Sunset Boulevard crosses
Gower as it travels westward,
lower right to upper left, through
the sprawling grounds of the
Christie Studios in September,
1922. Century Corporation, later
part of Twentieth Century Fox, is
on the southwest corner of
Sunset and Gower, occupied
today by a Thrifty Drug Store
shopping complex. The group of
buildings at lower right later
became Columbia Pictures
Corporation. [Marc Wanamaker-
Bison Archives] □

In 1913 the Christie Film Company advertised itself as "manufacturers of Nestor Comedies, Universal Films." Executives and some of the leading actors pose outside at Sunset and Gower for this company photograph. [Marc Wanamaker-Bison Archives] □

Below, the studios of William Horsley and H. Paulis on the south side of Sunset just east of Gower in 1921. Several movie production companies occupied these buildings over a 20-year period, with Columbia Pictures Corporation later taking over and expanding the facilities. Until

1976 Pathé News offices were in the Paulis building, while Jerry Fairbanks Short-Subjects Productions were in the Horsley offices. [Marc Wanamaker-Bison Archives] □

The Century Film Corporation in 1921 on the southwest corner of Sunset and Gower. The studios and sets covered almost half a block behind this front office building, used for administration and payroll. [Marc Wanamaker-Bison Archives] □

One of the earliest buildings on the historic corner of Sunset and Gower. This "6-Mile House" sat on the northeast corner in 1890, and served as a place for overnight lodging and meals. Gower is the narrow road running north at the far left of the photo. [Bruce Torrence Historical Collection, Pacific Federal Savings] ☐

Today's Palladium, about to be
remodeled by the Marriott
Corporation. □

More than 6,500 people gathered in the Hollywood Palladium for the opening night of Tex Beneke's Orchestra in 1947. [Leo Walker] ☐

Les Brown and His Band of Renown has delighted audiences for over forty years and still plays beautiful music from Hollywood to New York. The band has appeared many times in the Hollywood Palladium on Sunset Boulevard. ☐

100 cement blocks, weighing 100 pounds each, lined the outside wall of the Earl Carroll Theatre with "signatures of the stars" until they were taken down in the early 1960s. The first signatures were cast in wet cement, prompting a call from Sid Grauman, miffed that the idea was in direct competition with his famous Chinese Theatre's courtyard. Carroll relented, and thereafter signatures were painted onto the cement. Variety Arts Center received 60 of the legendary blocks and many of the others were purchased by Gene Autry, in anticipation of opening a museum. [Bruce Torrence Historical Collection, Pacific Federal Savings] □

116

Earl Carroll in 1937. The
entrepreneur was later killed in a
plane crash. [Variety Arts
Center] □

The fabulous Earl Carroll Theatre in 1944, across Sunset Boulevard from the Hollywood Palladium. Several of Carroll's "Beautiful Girls" became Hollywood stars. [Variety Arts Center] □

A small cover charge and $5.50 bought you dinner, wine, and a great show. [Variety Arts Center] □

119

Dismantling the old Hollywood
sign in 1978 to make way for the
new. Reconstruction was
facilitated by an energetic drive
by local citizens to save the
dilapidated landmark from
extinction. □

On a Sunday outing, this family pauses to be photographed at Sunset and Vine in 1901. Vine Street, called Weyse then, runs north just behind the carriage's rear wheels. The first full-length movie was filmed on this corner twelve years later. [Historical Collections, Security Pacific National Bank] □ Below, the famous corner as it appeared in 1930, with Vine Street to the left. From 1927 to 1932 it served as a used car lot. [Bruce Torrence Historical Collection, Pacific Federal Savings] □

What a difference 79 years can
make! Sunset and Vine, running
north at left, in 1980. □

This fabulous stained-glass
window at Sunset and Vine pays
tribute to filmdom's greats.
[Home Savings & Loan
Association] □

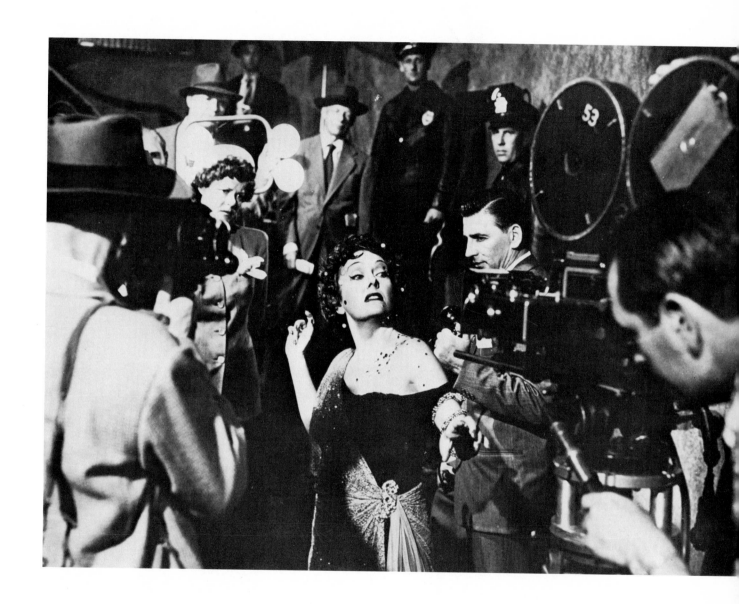

Gloria Swanson in her superb portrayal of Norma Desmond in *Sunset Boulevard*, the story of a silent screen actress living on the Boulevard in her own private dream-world until she finally murders her gigolo. In her heyday as a superstar Miss Swanson actually did reside on Sunset Strip in an opulent Spanish hacienda. One of her neighbors was Buster Keaton. [Paramount Pictures] □

As he skates along Vine Street a local youth views the sidewalk stars, as do thousands of tourists each year. The first stars were laid in January of 1961. To date, approximately 1,723 names are preserved in bronze to commemorate the greats of the entertainment world. The Merv Griffin Show is filmed in the building beneath the billboard at left. □

The late Los Angeles financier Howard Ahmanson, second from left, and Hollywood Chamber of Commerce officials preside over the lowering of a 1968 "time capsule" into the sidewalk at Sunset and Vine, "the most famous corner in the world." The lucite container preserves memorabilia from the radio, television and motion picture industries, to be dug up in the year 2004. A bronze plaque placed over the spot cites the corner as the birthplace of motion pictures and the symbol of the radio and television media. [Home Savings and Loan] □

Cecil B. DeMille directing an "indoor" scene of *The Squaw Man* at Sunset and Vine in December, 1913. Two movie greats, Samuel Goldwyn and Jesse Lasky, financed, produced, and distributed the film. Note the lemon grove in the background.

[Bruce Torrence Historical Collection, Pacific Federal Savings] ☐
The West Coast offices of Famous Players-Lasky Corporation in 1921, eight years after the first movie was filmed in Hollywood. This building, at

Sunset and Vine, was part of Paramount Pictures until Paramount moved to nearby Melrose Avenue two years later. [Marc Wanamaker-Bison Archives] ☐

Jake Stern's historic barn as it looked in 1929, sitting near where it was used in film making's earliest days. In the background is the then-new Taft Building and another high rise under construction two blocks away at Hollywood and Vine. [Los Angeles Public Library] □

Jake Stern's barn, once sitting in a small field on Vine Street just above Sunset, served as Hollywood's first enclosed stage when Cecil B. DeMille directed the first feature-length film in 1913. The barn was moved in 1927 to the Lasky Group's Paramount lot on Melrose Avenue, then in October of 1979 was moved back to Vine, opposite the famous Capitol Records building, where it will become a museum. These photos show the barn being hoisted from the Paramount lot, turning from the lot onto Melrose, crossing Sunset Boulevard, and finally placed near the Capitol Records building back on Vine Street. □

This 1944 photograph shows the huge NBC building at Sunset and Vine. During World War II long lines of servicemen on leave formed at the entrance to see live radio broadcasts. Television at that time was just gearing up for its big leap into the American home in the late forties. Note the Griffith Observatory on the hilltop at center. [Marc Wanamaker-Bison Archives] □

A large mural dominates the interior of the old NBC building at Sunset and Vine. The site is now occupied by a savings and loan office. [NBC] □

Famous radio personalities
Fibber McGee and Molly — Mr.
and Mrs. Jim Jordan — around
1940. [National Archives] □

Bob Hope, Frances Langford,
Jerry Colonna, and Ben Gage on
their famous "Pepsodent Show"
which ran on NBC from
September, 1938 to June, 1940.
[National Archives] □

Amos 'n' Andy — Freeman
Gosden and Charles Correll — at
the height of their radio career,
broadcasting in April, 1938 on
NBC. This was a publicity photo
for a newspaper article. [National
Archives] □

Popular singer Vic Damone in
a recording session at the NBC
studio in 1958. [NBC] □

The late Edgar Bergen and
Charlie McCarthy in a broadcast
for NBC's "Chase and Sanborn
Program" in May, 1937.
[National Archives] □

The NBC complex in 1952, showing Sunset Boulevard at extreme right and Vine running north from right to left in the center of the photo. The Hollywood Palladium, in the upper right corner, features Stan Kenton. Across the parking lot behind NBC is the RCA building. Jake Stern's barn stood approximately where the first row of cars is parked behind NBC. [NBC] □

Demolition of the huge NBC complex in May, 1964. Many of America's most popular radio programs were broadcast from these facilities for over three decades. Note the stars in the Vine Street sidewalk at extreme left. [Robert R. Jensen] □

Fountains, a reflecting pool and a marble sculpture by the Finnish-American artist Eino, grace Sunset and Vine today. □ Hollywood Cash Grocery, the first store in Hollywood, was attached to the rear of a residence in 1900 at the northeast corner of Sunset and Cahuenga Boulevards. In this 1905 photo Cahuenga is seen running north directly behind the buggy at the left. [The C.C. Pierce Collection] □

Danny Kaye was one of the many film and radio stars who volunteered countless hours to bring fun and laughter to servicemen who visited the Hollywood Canteen. Hundreds of thousands of military personnel stopped here to enjoy a week-end pass with the celebrities. The stars also helped serve food and beverages, and even did the dishes. Actress Linda Darnell once said, "The happiest moments of my life were the times when I entertained at the Hollywood Canteen...the smiles on those boys' faces were exhilarating!" [Bruce Torrence Historical Collection, Pacific Federal Savings] ☐

A haven for enlisted men during World War II, the renowned Hollywood Canteen offered food, entertainment and dancing. The famous club sat on Cahuenga just 150 feet south of Sunset where a three-level parking structure now stands. Dancing was divided into three shifts to accomodate the throngs of servicemen who lined up each night. Note the pre-integration lines of black soldiers on the left, white on the right. [Bruce Torrence Historical Collection, Pacific Federal Savings] □

Marie Wilson and Ken Murray
entertain servicemen with one of
their "blackout" skits at the
Hollywood Canteen. Jane
Russell was one of the founders
of the popular mecca exclusively
for enlisted personnel. [Bruce
Torrence Historical Collection,
Pacific Federal Savings] □

Long lines are common outside the unique Cinerama Dome Theatre on the south side of Sunset Boulevard at Ivar. In the early 1900s a mansion with a large garden stood here. □ Below, the sign on the roof of this building was the first electric sign in Hollywood. P.F. Pursel and Son livery stable was on the south side of Sunset near Wilcox Avenue. Photo was taken in 1910. [Bruce Torrence Historical Collection, Pacific Federal Savings] □

144

In 1937 the Hollywood Athletic Club, on the north side of Sunset near Wilcox, was the place for filmdom's elite to keep in shape. Edgar Bergen was a member; Charlie McCarthy was an honorary member. [Los Angeles Public Library] □

Hollywood's "new" Chamber of Commerce building was completed in 1926 and still stands, though presently occupied by a camera store, across Sunset from the Athletic Club. The famous Westmore Brothers later opened their make-up studios a block away. [Bruce Torrence Historical Collection, Pacific Federal Savings] □

An appropriate inscription for Sunset Boulevard adorns the Caroline Leonetti building. □

Klieglights pierce the sky as downtown Hollywood bathes in another premier. Sunset and Hollywood Boulevards run parallel, left to right, hidden by the hilltop. [Historical Collections, Security Pacific National Bank] □

In 1905 Hollywood High School accomodated fewer than 100 students. Later graduates include Lana Turner, Natalie Wood and Carol Burnett. [C.C. Pierce Collection] □

Each an anachronism to the other, the 1930s art-deco tower of Crossroads of the World rises next to the traditional spire of the Blessed Sacrament Church, both on Sunset Boulevard near Las Palmas, practically in the heart of Hollywood. □

Courtyard of Crossroads of the
World, a complex of offices, each
unique in design, such as the
ship motif in the background. □

Looking west on Sunset Boulevard at Highland in 1922, with a portion of Hollywood High School visible at the right. [Historical Collections, Security Pacific National Bank] □

Sunset and Highland, today a major intersection, shows the remodeled "Holly High" at the right. Note the growth of palm trees. □

GRAND OPENING
OCT. 15 '76
★★★★
HOLLYWOOD
DISCO
7000
★★★
HOLLYWOOD
ROOSEVELT HOTEL
7000 HOLLYWOOD BLVD.
FOR INFORMATION CALL 273-4106

Dodge

MAP
TO
STAR
HOME

A budding entrepreneur
peddles his wares near the
Hollywood High School campus. □

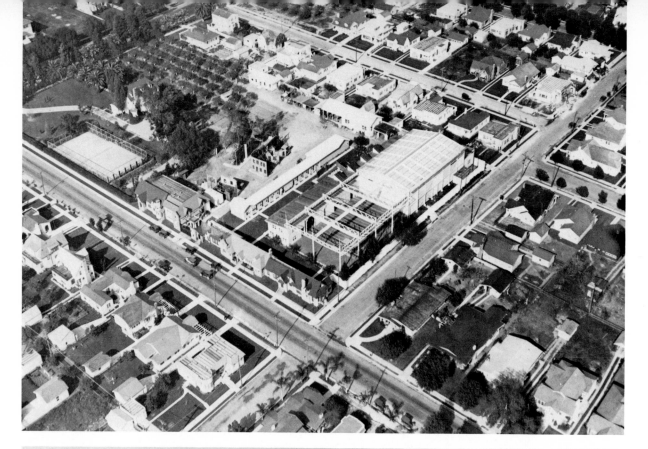

Charlie Chaplin's home among the trees in the upper left in 1922, with the tennis court facing Sunset. Behind his home are the studios he built on La Brea Avenue. [Bruce Torrence Historical Collection, Pacific Federal Savings] □

Charlie Chaplin directed most of his own films, such as *The Circus,* shown here. [A & M Records] □

The world's all-time comedy
genius in a scene from *The Gold
Rush*, filmed in 1925. [Authors'
Collection] ☐
The Kid, a 1921 silent film.
[Authors' Collection] ☐

A light snow falls on La Brea Avenue in front of the Tyrolean-style Chaplin Studios in 1920. [Marc Wanamaker-Bison Archives] ☐

Below, the entry to A & M Records, formerly the Charlie Chaplin Studios. The record company is co-owned by Herb Alpert, the famous trumpeter of the Tijuana Brass. ☐

154

Los Angeles Mayor Tom Bradley, right, appears at the installation of Herb Alpert's star in the Hollywood "Walk of Fame." Alpert appeared on numerous occasions at the Hollywood Palladium [A & M Records] ☐

Tiny Naylor's Drive-In, on the exact spot where the famous Carpenter's Drive-In stood in the days when a beef sandwich and milkshake cost about 30 cents. At Sunset and La Brea near the Chaplin Studios, it is one of Southern California's few remaining drive-ins. ☐

The A.Z. Taft home on Sunset at Ogden, just east of Fairfax Avenue. Built in 1900 and occupied by the family until recently, the home has been recommended as an historical monument by the city's Cultural Board. The Tafts constructed a large downtown office building at the corner of Hollywood and Vine. ☐

Cyclists take a break in front of the Preview House on Sunset west of Gardner. Prospective television programs are viewed here by a pre-selected audience, chosen from the general public, before shows are sold to sponsors and scheduled for airing. A well-kept 15-room mansion stood on this site until 1963. □

Noontime traffic at Sunset and Gardner, looking east toward downtown Hollywood, in July of 1927. A Pacific Electric "red car" crosses Sunset to cut through a residential area on its way to Santa Monica Boulevard, the direct route to the beaches. The building at right was one of the first two-story commercial structures built in Hollywood. [Bruce Torrence Historical Collection, Pacific Federal Savings] □

Sunset and Gardner today. Note the buildings at the edges of the photograph are also in the 1927 photo. □

Street improvements are made on Sunset Boulevard near Highland in 1907. Lemon and orange groves lined the Boulevard until about 1915. Are the women in the background wives with lunch? [Historical Collections, Security Pacific National Bank] □

The lovely C.F. Harper home stood above Sunset just east of Laurel Canyon Boulevard. The house was built in 1897 and photographed here in 1905. Harper was a citrus farmer and one of the first settlers in Hollywood. He later sub-divided his land and made a fortune in real estate. Today on Sunset, just below the orange grove in the foreground, stands the famous Schwab's Drug Store. Harper Street runs north-south nearby. [Bruce Torrence Historical Collection, Pacific Federal Savings] □

Donn Arden's
MGM GRAND HOTEL
LAS VEGAS
UNIVERSITY
STEREO
FRONTIER HOTEL
LAS VEGAS
MAY 7-13
YANX
ARCO
134

THE STRIP
Sunset's Golden Era

The throngs of servicemen have dwindled; today only a handful show up for conducted tours at television stations or stand in line to be seated at the popular network shows. Other visitors, though, including servicemen from other countries, descend on the Strip every week for brief sightseeing jaunts. But they don't find the same two-mile section of the Boulevard they would have found in the thirties, forties, or even the fifties. There are still remnants of that fabled glamour born in the thirties, but its landmark nightclubs — The Mocambo, Ciro's, The Trocadero, The Clover Club, The Marquis, La Rue, and The Players Club — are no more. Today its glamour emanates from noisy discotheques, small theatres, unique gourmet restaurants, strip joints, health food eateries, luxurious offices, stores and boutiques for the young and rich, recording studios, high-rise apartments and condominiums, antique parlors containing fortunes in ancient furniture and bric-a-brac, art and ceramic galleries, interior decorators' impressive showrooms, architects' display foyers, hotels, sidewalk cafes *a la Parisienne*, and classy Mexican cantinas.

Many offices of movie stars' agents remain, and perhaps that's where our story of the Golden Era should begin, for it was primarily the "agent industry" that built the Strip and established its fame. Those magical few who managed the personal and professional lives of the stars were once the street's major tenants. From its very beginning, where it takes off from the former Garden of Allah and veers to the left at the little roadway leading to the old Chateau Marmont apartment-hotel, the Strip has always been lined with agents' offices, their waiting room walls covered with elegantly framed sepia photos of star-clients. The size of the photos characteristically matched the fame of the clients — the images of really *big* stars' photos were usually blown up to the size of giant posters,

most of the earlier ones having been done by Max Munn Autry or Walter Seeley, whose posh salon sat next door to the Marquis restaurant back in the thirties. Near Seeley's photographic salon were sprinkled a few studios of prominent vocal and drama coaches, including Beulah Hartz, Madame Maria Ouspenskaya (who herself acted in movies on the side), and Josephine Dillon, Clark Gable's first wife, who later moved into a quaint thatched-roof cottage on Highland just off Sunset. (Three leaner decades later Miss Dillion's debts and mortgage on her house were paid off by Gable.)

Some agents built their own offices; others leased suites from rich landlords who'd bought up Strip land as fast as they could negotiate it. Several of these landlords were stars who sensed good real estate bargains and grabbed them. One successful agent even rented a luxurious suite from one of his own star-clients. The Talmadge sisters, Constance and Norma, were probably the most well-known landladies along the Strip. Until just recently the Norma Talmadge Building stood at 8720 Sunset Boulevard. The sisters built it in 1929 with income from their own careers and investments made by their mother. Upon previewing a newly released "talkie" the sisters had made in 1929, Norma wired her sister in New York: "Our voices are so bad, the picture is so awful, we should call it quits and thank God for the trust fund Mother set up for us." Talking pictures spelled the end of their careers, but both died very rich. The La Dome Restaurant now takes the place of the old Talmadge building at 9000 Sunset.

Stars wooed from the New York stage by hopeful producers, or Broadway players who came to Hollywood seeking an agent to launch their film careers, usually landed at the Garden of Allah, the Chateau Marmont, or at more modest quarters back near Highland. The well-heeled would settle in at the Sunset Tower Apartments, perched high on the brink of the Strip overlooking vast flatlands below, where tree-lined avenues criss-cross Sunset from the Plaza to Beverly Hills. The east windows offer spacious views of Wilshire Boulevard, La Cienega, Santa Monica Boulevard, San Vicente, Doheny, Olympic, Pico, and Melrose Avenue. This old apartment-hotel, remodeled, redecorated, and expensively furnished, still stands. Billie Burke occupied an apartment there for several years and it was the home of actress Irene Rich, one of the original tenants, for forty years.

The grand Chateau Marmont, though, attracted most of the important out-of-towners. This great house still stands proudly at the foot of a lovely hill on the gateway to the Strip, adjacent to the former Players Club. Dowdy and time-worn, yet elegant and dignified, the aging Queen Mother has hosted Hollywood and Broadway "nobility" — along with crowned heads of real European houses — for over five decades. Copied from a French chateau in the Loire Valley and built in 1926, its high hedges and thick walls have sheltered some of the biggest names in show business. On her trips to Hollywood Greta Garbo hid out at the Marmont — "the only hotel in America where birds sang on my window sill" — following her self-exile from publicity. It was her favorite hotel on the West Coast, where she always registered as Miss Brown. For years rumors claimed that she once owned the hostelry, but no deeds substantiate the story. Jean Harlow spent her honeymoon there, and the management still maintains her suite exactly as it was then. Gertrude Lawrence resided there on two occasions, as did Fanny Brice. Two members of the Vanderbilt family chose to stay at the chateau in preference to the noisy, busy hotels in Los Angeles or Beverly Hills, and famous pantomimist Marcel Marceau, on his trips to America, used to check into the sturdy old inn. Myrna Loy once remarked, "The greatest thing about the Marmont is its privacy ... each guest respects the privacy of every other guest ... it's lovely." On his first trip to Hollywood Laurence Olivier registered at the Marmont, and Sophia Loren stayed there briefly and fell in love with the old place. Part of The Music Man was composed by Meredith Willson in a room on the second floor, and Los Angeles police files indicate that Howard Hughes went into seclusion at the hotel for two years in the early fifties. His closely guarded suites — three in all — were adjacent to one rented by Boris Karloff, who made the Marmont his home for many years.

In later years some of its residents have been John Lennon of The Beatles, along with his wife, Yoko, Dustin Hoffman while filming The Graduate, Paul Newman and Joanne Woodward, Maximillian Schell, and rock star Mick Jagger. One evening just prior to a televised Academy Awards presentation at the Santa Monica Civic Auditorium, Patricia Neal, Melvyn Douglas, Martin Balsam, and Sidney Portier all checked in simultaneously, and returned in the early morning hours — each with an Oscar!

By the early thirties dozens of agents occupied offices along the Strip. One of the first was Leon Lance, who represented many of Hollywood's top stars. He "discovered" James Arness and plugged away for parts for the young actor just returning from World War II, but Arness later signed with a larger agency. Another early agent was Bessie Loo, who specialized in handling Asian actors and musicians; Bessie is still doing business on the Strip. Carlos Alvarado specializes in Latin actors, but also represents a few others who appear in television commercials. Many of the larger agencies — among them, the William Morris Agency, Burton Moss, Howard King, Mitchell J. Hamilburg, and the Leaverton Associates — have moved to newer quarters away from Sunset. They're now in Beverly Hills, Century City, or along La Cienega and Wilshire boulevards. Some of the active agencies still found on Sunset Strip are Grace Lyons, Lola Moore, the Mishkin Agency, the Hiller Agency, Carter J. Gibson, the Goldfarb-Lewis Agency, Jerry B. Wheeler Associates, and Don Schwartz. The 1976 edition of the Pacific Coast Studio Directory lists no fewer than 310 agents in the Southern California area, most of them on the Strip. Collectively they do a multi-million dollar business — and retain ten per cent of their clients' astronomical salaries.

Some stars, as their fame and pocketbooks swelled, bought homes along Sunset Strip — on the fashionable north side where the hills rise sharply and offer a splendid view. A notable exception was John Barrymore. Upon arriving in Hollywood he leased a small bungalow on the south edge near La Cienega for a bargain price. Nestled near it, down a slight slope, was a tiny two-room guest house. Robert Taylor occupied this house as Barrymore's guest for about a year; Errol Flynn rented it later. Today the two houses comprise the quaint Butterfield Restaurant, a health food eatery and mecca for writers. Mickey Rooney bought a home for himself and his parents on the north side of the Strip, up the hill from

Barrymore's place. Farther west near Doheny famed comedian Buster Keaton purchased a Spanish-style home, and above Keaton's, on a high plateau, stood the home of character actress Gale Sondergaard, whose career almost died under the scandalous investigations of Senator Joe McCarthy. Silent screen star Mae Marsh built a mansion on Larabee Street, three blocks off the Strip. So did Henry B. Walthall, another star of the silent screen, remembered particularly for his performance in *Birth of a Nation.*

The original owners of this land, of course, were Mexican *dons* who came northward to petition for land grants when Pio Pico and his predecessors governed California. They in turn sold chunks of their ranchos to *gringos* who came from the East Coast, from small farms in the Midwest, or who immigrated from Europe to find new homes on America's sunny coast. One of these was Belgian immigrant Victor Ponet, who served as his country's consul in Los Angeles. In 1890 he purchased 240 acres of the remaining portion of Rancho La Brea. The heart of that property is the heart of Sunset Strip. Ponet's grandson, Francis S. Montgomery, began to develop that portion known as the Sunset Plaza in 1924 and gave it the *Champs Elysee* look. He also subdivided large residential areas on which huge mansions and imposing apartment houses were eventually built. Much of this property was later rezoned to commercial lots and sold to investors such as Bob and Bing Crosby, the Talmadge sisters, Loretta Young, Fred MacMurray, Eddie Cantor, Preston Sturges, and Norma Shearer.

On the Ponet property were built some of the most famous restaurants in America — all on Sunset Strip. Billy Wilkerson built Ciro's and The Mocambo. (Today his widow, Tichi Wilkerson Miles, is the editor of fildom's famous newspaper, the *Hollywood Reporter.*) Preston Sturges built Players Club. Now a popular Japanese restaurant, the Players was a favorite of Marlene Dietrich, who usually resided at the nearby Chateau Marmont. Then along came the Trocadero, Marquis, La Rue, The Clover Club, and finally, in the fifties and sixties, The Cock 'n' Bull, Scandia, The Villanova, Crescendo, Galaxy, Melody Room, and Pandora's Box. Late-comers were Whiskey a Go Go, Dino's (the much-photographed night club in television's "77 Sunset Strip"), The Jerry Lewis Restaurant, The Scene, It's Boss, P.J.'s, Gazzarri's, and Cyrano. America's greatest bands, rock groups, and recording stars appeared at one time or another in these famous eateries, and

some of the finest chefs in the world prepared the menus.

Some of these restaurants have disappeared — torn down for high-rise construction or converted to discotheques, several shoddy in design and decor. Lovers of elegant Russian food have said goodby to the famous old *Bublichki.* Tucked away behind a small parking lot on Sunset at Larabee, it was one of those replaced by a high-rise office building. No other Russian restaurant in Southern California over the past thirty-five years has equalled the *Bublichki* in old-world elegance, atmosphere and genuine Russian cuisine. Two famous chains, Carpenter's and Dolores', operated drive-in restaurants on the north side of Sunset not far from La Cienega Boulevard. The drive-ins are all but extinct — plans are now under way to demolish the one remaining Dolores' down on Wilshire Boulevard. Several other eateries appeared on Sunset Strip, were much talked about, then disappeared just as suddenly as they came. The short-lived Telephone Booth, the Sea Witch, and The Trip fell into this category, as did The Jerry Lewis Restaurant, which soon became The Classic Cat, a plush topless cafe. About the only restaurant to achieve institution status along the Strip is the perennially popular Scandia.

At the height of the Vietnam War hundreds of hippies descended on Sunset Strip, handing out flowers and anti-war pamphlets to passersby and motorists paused at traffic signals. Clusters of long-haired hitchhikers stood at every major corner, most of them hitching rides into Hollywood — only to hitch right back to the Strip again — or westward to their campsites at the beach. During those tumultuous years police almost weekly quelled anti-war riots, and landlords found themselves replacing expensive storefront windows shattered during the melees. "Make Love, Not War" resounded along Sunset, and the peace demonstrators formed campsites right in the middle of sidewalks or in walkways between buildings — sleeping there, eating there, and making love, not war. Why the sudden influx of flower children and the ensuing anti-war riots occurred at the very heart of Sunset Strip will probably never be known. The episode temporarily marred its glitter, but the seventies saw a return to business-as-usual, oddly marked by the opening of a pornographic bookstore and cinema, the latest form of entertainment to hit the Strip.

The riots and porno shops didn't shock the old-timers — after all, there'd been nude entertainment and topless bars for nearly ten years — not to mention murders, rapes, gang fights in the thirties, gambling, and nightclub brawls. Fists were even swinging at the swankiest cafes. Remember Bugsy Siegel? Mickey Cohen? Tony Moreno from Mexico? George Raft's friends? And big Guy McAfee, the former Los Angeles vice squad officer? Sunset Strip was their West Coast headquarters. More than one gangland beating and a Mafia-connected murder took place on the Strip — practically under the nose of the Hollywood Police Department. Moreno's gambling parties netted him a fortune, which he neatly tucked away in Mexican banks. Siegel was gunned down by a hit man; Cohen died following a lengthy prison term.

Today a second golden era is coming to Sunset Strip. The popular recording industry earns hundreds of millions of dollars annually for its promoters. Giant billboards tower above the street proclaiming America's latest superstars and their hits. In finely painted blazing colors, these King-Kong-sized idols gaze down on the mere mortals who've pushed them to the top. With incomes soaring above the million-dollar mark, the new breed of superstar is reviving the Midas touch of bygone days — and the Strip heralds their fame.

Sunset Strip is home to former Beatle Ringo Starr, his seventeen-room mansion overlooking the gargantuan billboards. When asked recently by a *Los Angeles Times* reporter why he chose the Strip over Beverly Hills or Bel-Air, Starr replied, "I've always lived along Sunset Boulevard ... that's Hollywood to me, the images of it from my childhood....I don't want a house in Bel-Air or anywhere else...."

Below Starr's home strippers perform dead-sex at the new 77 Sunset Strip or the Body Shop. Tourists and conventioneers pour into the nearby Hotel Continental, then head for the skin clubs. Every day Ben Frank's spacious coffee shop hosts hundreds of teenagers, sightseers, and eccentric transients. A very noisy, busy place on weekends and evenings, Frank's has been there for years. Says the manager, philosophically, "We get all types — but we love 'em all!"

The finer hostels and apartments appear on the western end of Sunset Strip, where the Boulevard dips and curves into opulent Beverly Hills. Shiny new office structures, some as high as sixteen stories, sit alongside these hotels. This western end sees less hustle-and-bustle. Businessmen and apartment residents move quietly from mosaic-lined lobbies into waiting taxis — no milling clumps of young people, no tourists with cameras, no flashing neons. Sunset Strip ends here, where the transition into Beverly Hills is barely perceptible. As one leaves the Strip, the question lingers: Has this been a myth? Is Sunset Strip the Boulevard's fantasyland? A mere fable? Not identified on any official map, not listed in any ledger, not printed on any computer card at City Hall, and — except for the fictional "77 Sunset Strip" — not even an address, it is only an area, a part of Sunset Boulevard with a story all its own. Fashionable, seedy, exotic, or even depressing, Sunset Strip is somehow aristocratic, from the old-world Chateau Marmont to that supple curve in the road where a quiet sign reads: Beverly Hills.

Occasionally hot winds combined with dry brush spark hillside fires like this one burning dangerously close to Sunset Strip. Eleven mansions were recently destroyed here by such a blaze. □

Building sites are graded along Sunset Boulevard in 1905. This view, looking west from Fairfax Avenue, is just three streets east of where the famous Schwab's Drug Store was to be built 22 years later. [Los Angeles Public Library] □

Once an 18-foot wide drug store with a tiny prescription counter at the rear, Schwab's has enjoyed fame since 1930 as "the" spot on Sunset for celebrities to meet for coffee. The left half of the store (to the left of the couple standing on the sidewalk) was a fruit and vegetable store before the building was remodeled. Although never substantiated, the rumor persists that some lucky stars were "discovered" while working at Schwab's. □

168

A streetcar pauses for passengers on Sunset at Laurel Canyon in 1908. Today the entry to Schwab's parking lot is located just about where the sidewalk appears in the lower left corner of the photograph. Note the C.F. Harper residence in the distance. [Bruce Torrence Historical Collection, Pacific Federal Savings.] □

Below, a 1954 view of the Spanish-style bungalow where Alla Nazimova lived. The silent screen star built the hotel one block from Schwab's and named it the Garden of Allah. Character actress Edna Mae Oliver, remembered primarily for *Oliver Twist*, occupied a small bungalow here for many years until her death in 1959. Author Robert Benchley, whose son Peter wrote the novel *Jaws*, lived here for ten years. The world-famous hotel was home to many stars of the silent era through the 1930s and '40s. [Bruce Torrence Historical Collection, Pacific Federal Savings] □

Rolls Royces and billboards saluting
recording artists herald the Strip's
second golden era. □

The beautiful Chateau Marmont, one of the most famous buildings in Hollywood, marks the beginning of Sunset Strip. Just two blocks from Schwab's Drug Store, the internationally known hotel has hosted some of the world's greatest entertainment figures as well as royalty from numerous countries. The mysterious billionaire Howard Hughes kept three suites of rooms here. □

Elegant Gothic arches grace the entrance to the Chateau Marmont. Betty Grable checked in here when she first arrived in Hollywood. Marilyn Monroe stayed at the Marmont while filming *Bus Stop*, her room just down the hall from Jean

Harlow's honeymoon suite, which is still maintained as it was then. □
Carmen Miranda once remarked that the Chateau Marmont was "too beautiful for words." Here in the compact, old-world lobby Debra Paget met

her friends for coffee klatches. Guests in the late 20s frequently observed silent star John Gilbert being escorted, inebriated, to the exit. The piano supporting the bouquet in the foreground was used for rehearsals by part of the cast of *Hair* in the late 1960s. □

SUNSET TOWER

LUXURY APARTMENTS
AVAILABLE

A fading glory, the landmark Sunset Tower Apartments rise above the Strip. Many stars have resided here, including Carole Landis and Zasu Pitts. Famed gangster "Bugsy" Siegel lived here until asked by the management to leave. □

A publicity shot of Gloria
Swanson, released world-wide to
promote *Sunset Boulevard* in
1949. [Paramount Pictures] □

Hollywood's visibly rich dined at the luxurious Trocadero on the Strip. The cafe was a favorite of Joan Crawford, Veronica Lake and singer Frances Langford.

[Historical Collection, Security Pacific National Bank] ☐

The Mocambo, featuring Eartha Kitt in 1953, was one of eight popular restaurants on Sunset Strip frequented by movie clientele in the '40s and '50s. It was Errol Flynn's favorite night spot. [Bruce Torrence Historical Collection, Pacific Federal Savings] □

A typical scene along Sunset Strip. The Ponet residence is in the background to left of center, and Beatle Ringo Starr's home is out of the picture at left, hidden behind trees. □

Sunset Strip was paved from Havenhurst to Horn Avenue in 1931 and the eastern portion is shown here in 1934. Clockwise from top are 1:Avocado groves. 2:The Ponet estate. This house was built in 1924 by Francis S. Montgomery. 3:The Baker house, which became the Clover Club in 1938. 4:The home of Dr. Mensur, which became the Colony Club in 1937. Both the Clover Club and the Colony Club featured gambling. 5:The Trocadero Cafe. 6:The vacant lot where the Eagles Cafe, featuring Russian cuisine, had been. Charlie Chaplin was dining there the night it burned down in 1928. 7:The point, still there, marking the entrance to Sunset Plaza Drive. 8:St. Victor's Church, built by Victor Ponet in 1906. 9:Original poinsettia fields of Paul Ecke, the largest grower and shipper of poinsettias in the U.S. Located now in Encinitas near San Diego, Ecke established his fields here in 1920 and also had fields near Sunset and Doheny Drive in Beverly Hills. [Marc Wanamaker-Bison Archives] □

Cliff says he gives the best
tattoos in town! He set up his
parlor on the south side of the
Strip in a former real estate
office. □

Ciro's Night Club, one of the best known in its day, has become The Comedy Store. Established comedians come here to test new material before a live audience, while new talent hopes to be noticed by an agent or television producer. ☐

Below, tourists gather at the entrance of a sidewalk cafe. The Strip features many of these cafes, giving it a European flavor. ☐

A popular Sunset Strip disco-
teque near Doheny Drive. □

Promotion posters line the exterior of a major record outlet on Sunset near San Vicente Boulevard. Today the Strip is a nucleus for album production and promotion for America's insatiable pop music buffs. ☐

Whiskey a Go Go, a well-known night club, opened in the mid 60s and was visited frequently by the Beatles whenever they passed through Hollywood. Ringo Starr lives nearby. ☐

Gazzarri's attracts young adults who prefer "soft rock" bands. ☐

These three popular night spots
typify the Strip's offerings. □

BEVERLY HILLS
The Money Kingdom

America's Dream Street comes into its own in Beverly Hills. Barely a quarter-mile longer than the Strip, this stretch of Sunset Boulevard is the most glamorous, touching upon the northern edge of a city famed for its wealthy inhabitants, mansions, Garden-of-Eden roadways and parks, and its powerful financial institutions. You know almost instinctively you're in Beverly Hills. Immediately on your right as you leave the Strip, half hidden behind a stone wall and perfectly trimmed shrubbery, looms a magnificent mansion. The sidewalks and curbs — even the gutters — are spotless; a weedless, bumpless, patchless carpet of green flows down to meet the wall. The house next door is even larger, a veritable palace lifted out of the hills of Lichtenstein and plunked down on Sunset Boulevard to cast its fairy-tale shadow onto slim palms and flowery acacias. And then another, and another — all homes of the very, very rich.

Above these, on shelves sliced into the hills by land developers in the thirties, are more castles, copied from the finest of Bavaria, England, and those along the Rhine.

Prior to 1925 this exquisite neighborhood was mostly farmland, with ravines and barrancas cutting deep into the hillside soil. In rainy seasons the ravines gushed floodwaters onto the flatlands below, causing a massive muddy lake. Beverly Hills was formerly a Spanish land grant and the mid nineteenth century saw cattle and sheep grazing on the ranch of Maria Valdez. Following a bitter feud with her cousin Luciano over watering spots for the herds, Maria sold off part of her inherited ranch. Soon after the sale her husband suddenly died, leaving her with eleven children. She then sold the remainder of the ranch, vacated her house near the corner of present-day Sunset Boulevard and Alpine Drive, and moved into a smaller house in downtown Los Angeles near the Plaza. Maria's land went from subdivision to sub-

division, from her first buyer, Benito Wilson, to the year 1907, when smaller lots became available to hundreds of settlers. Streets were laid out from Sunset Boulevard, real estate offices popped up everywhere, and money-in-hand buyers — investors, lenders, developers, craftsmen, merchants — rushed in. The little town thrived, mansions appeared along Sunset, and Maria's serene rancho, originally sold for a few thousand dollars, became the Money Kingdom.

Testimony to this influx is the great home of Max Whittier, a wealthy oilman and an original Beverly Hills developer. One of the first seen upon leaving the Strip, the Italian Renaissance-style mansion had no money spared in landscaping and interior furnishings. Until recently it was one of the largest, most handsome in all of Southern California. Early in 1978, however, the home was purchased by a young Saudi Arabian prince and his nineteen-year-old wife. They made drastic changes in the interior and exterior design, altering the landscaping, encrusting the walls and enclosed terraces with shells and glass, and offensively painting the lawn statuary. Soon after, the prince's father ordered him back to his homeland and the mansion was left in a shambles. Fire gutted it a few months later, and the once-lovely Max Whittier home was reduced to an ugly shell.

Nearby is the huge Roland Bishop mansion, just one block off Sunset, directly behind the Beverly Hills Hotel. The residence was later purchased from Bishop by banker Irving Hellman, who was one of Los Angeles' first real estate lenders. High on a cliff overlooking Sunset is the spacious mansion of Kirk B. Johnson, one of the founders of the Pioneer Oil Company (long since absorbed by a major oil firm) and an original Beverly Hills developer. The home, built in 1912, was remodeled in the late 1940s, and now can barely be glimpsed from Sunset behind groves of stately eucalyptus. Directly below is the palatial townhouse of industrialist and financier Francis Betiller, who chose the Sunset Boulevard site for his West Coast residence. These four palaces stand just half a mile from the little crossroads marking the location of Maria Valdez's modest adobe. Nearby, almost adjacent to Sunset Boulevard, are the homes of industrialists, financiers, wealthy merchants, retired East Coast millionaires, and dozens of movie stars, including Peter Falk, Loretta Young, Sammy Davis, Jr., Danny Thomas, Dinah Shore, Alice Faye, Victor Borge, Fred Astaire, George Burns, Red Skelton, and earlier, Richard Barthelmess, Marion Davies, Claudette Colbert, Tom Mix (after moving from Echo Park), Wallace Beery, Conrad Nagel, Jeanette MacDonald, and others. These lots jumped in price from about $850 in 1925 to $50,000 by 1929, and their proximity to the famous Beverly Hills Hotel kept their prices rising.

The Rodeo Land and Water Company, which had formed to subdivide part of Maria's land and to provide water for its inhabitants, built the hotel in 1912 to attract wealthy visitors from the East and Midwest. It was a gamble. With several fine hotels in Los Angeles and the famous Hollywood Hotel in downtown Hollywood, would visitors travel all the way "out to the country" where many lots still stood vacant, where sheep still grazed in the Coldwater Canyon hills, and where the tiny business center boasted barely a dozen stores? Who would run this great hotel? The directors decided on the remarkable Mrs. Margaret Anderson — noted throughout California as "the woman who *really* knows how to run a hotel" — and enticed her away from the Hollywood Hotel. But the immensely popular manageress drove a hard bargain. She demanded a handsome salary and asked for an option to buy the building when it became available. Aware of her business savvy and her reputation for supervising an efficient staff, company officials quickly agreed to her salary demands and even to the purchase option. The ambitious Mrs. Anderson later did buy the hotel and within a year turned it into a profitable operation — until 1929. Just eight months ahead of the crippling stock market crash she sold the hotel to a group of investors. In November of that year — eighteen years after its grand opening — the Beverly Hills Hotel closed its doors and kept them closed until 1933.

Using borrowed money, its new owners opened the doors once again with a publicity promotion that reached around the world. Within weeks the great hotel was putting out its welcome mat to the world's elite — the rich, the powerful, the glamorous, the noble. Some residents occupied spacious suites in two slim wings jutting out from each side of the main section almost parallel to Sunset. Others occupied cozy cottages strung casually along lawns and azalea beds at the rear. Things haven't changed. The *grand dame* of hotels remains solidly booked almost every day of the year, both in the main section and in the cottages. Though some guests tarry for as long as a year, others — celebrities, tycoons, and well-heeled tourists pop in and out as though scurrying through a busy airport lounge on a holiday weekend.

One of the hotel's attractions, even for "outsider" guests, is the famous Polo Lounge. Once a children's dining room — one of Mrs. Anderson's innovations — it is now a fashionable cocktail lounge hosting a swarm of guests from noon till closing time. The rich come here; movie and television aspirants come; also directors, producers, writers, stars, and tourists. They mix, they talk, they laugh, they argue, they drink. The bar had no name in the beginning. Polo was a popular game around Southern California in the mid twenties and Will Rogers, Darryl Zanuck, Randolph Scott, Walter Wanger, and other members of the Polo Club would drop in after chukkers to relax and discuss their game — hence earning its nickname. Polo is no longer discussed. Today the popular topic is, "How do we make a million in Hollywood?"

The movie industry was booming at the time of the hotel's reawakening. Beverly Hills boomed. More luxurious homes arose long Sunset reaching a mile around the bend beyond the great hotel, toward the Bel-Air district. Up went gargantuan Moroccan-style and English Tudor homes that mingled with copied Swiss chateaus, Roman temples, Spanish haciendas, and Georgian plantation mansions.

The Pacific Electric Railway had purchased right-of-way down the middle of Sunset and laid tracks, intending to bring rail service west to Santa Monica, but the idea was scrapped and by the early 1920s the clay strip and tracks near the hotel had been abandoned. What was to be done about this blight on the breathtaking beauty of Beverly Hills? Once more the creative prowess of Mrs. Anderson went to work. The wealthy locals loved their prize horses, and what better place to ride, to see, and be seen than down the middle of Sunset Boulevard, in front of the Beverly Hills Hotel? Along with her husband and financier Irving Hellman, Mrs. Anderson proposed that a bridle path be established along the right-of-way, beginning at Rodeo Drive. The three organized the Beverly Hills Bridle Path Association. Several prominent citizens — among them, movie-maker Milton Goetz, oilman Max Whittier and humorist Will Rogers — helped finance the path and set up a fund to maintain it in compliance with city ordinances. The path of decomposed granite, hedged with colorful shrubs, turned down Rodeo Drive; eastward it reached almost back to Doheny Drive near the western end of the Strip. It fostered even greater local interest in horseback riding and eventually became a tourist attraction. But it is there no more. The last remnants disappeared right after World War II when the city scraped up the granite surface, removed the hedges and laid in their place a landscaped strip of curbed lawn.

Sunset's heavy traffic had spelled the demise of the bridle path.

The Dream Street winds on. Its south curb touches Westwood; its north, Bel-Air, the enclave of the *superrich*: Cary Grant, Randolph Scott, the family of Louis B. Mayer, the Doheny family, Irene Dunne, Carol Burnett, the late Mary Pickford, and others. To the left, students traverse the vast campus of the University of California, while across the Boulevard to the right are high, ornate iron gates, fourteen-foot-high stone walls, planter boxes, and flower beds below towering eucalyptus and crepe myrtle trees. This is the fairy-tale entrance to the mecca of scores of America's multi-millionaires — the quiet, verdant hills of Bel-Air.

The former Max Whittier mansion, now burned out and boarded up. It was gutted by a fire soon after being vacated by a Saudi Arabian prince in 1978. □

A streetcar is about to head
eastward on Sunset in front of
the imposing Beverly Hills Hotel
in 1920. Note the encroachment
of private residences upon the
rural landscape beyond the hotel
at the right. The park in the
foreground still exists. [Title
Insurance and Trust Company] □

At right, the entrance to the
Beverly Hills Hotel today, where
a new wing was added in the
1940s. Six full-time gardeners
keep the grounds in immaculate
condition. Directly behind the
hotel is the huge residence of the
late newspaper mogul William
Randolph Hearst. □

Anne Baxter, Raymond
Massey at the Beverly Hills
Hotel. ☐

196

Loretta Young and director
George Cukor at a Beverly Hills
charity benefit. ☐

197

Photographer Ansel Adams at
a Beverly Hills press conference. ☐

The famous Beverly Hills bridle
path ran down the middle of
Sunset Boulevard, then
southward to Santa Monica
Boulevard in 1938. Riders pacing
their steeds became a common
sight for Sunday afternoon
motorists. [Marc Wanamaker-
Bison Archives] □

The Christie family in front of their home, Waverly, on Sunset Boulevard at Hillcrest Drive in 1928. Al and Charles Christie made their fortune from two- and three-reeler silents near Sunset and Gower back in Hollywood. Note the Scottish and wirehaired terriers, very popular pets of the day. [Marc Wanamaker-Bison Archives] □

Each Beverly Hills residence
seems to out-do the other. This
home on Sunset Boulevard near
the Beverly Hills Hotel is typical. ☐

In a scene typical of Beverly Hills, a tourist bus turns down palm-lined Camden Drive off Sunset. □

A German Regency-style
mansion faces Sunset near the
Beverly Hills Hotel. This is one of
the "smaller" homes that line the
Boulevard. □

The greystone mansion of the oil-rich Doheny family on Doheny Drive in 1928. The family made additional fortunes in real estate and have been benefactors to the University of Southern California over the years. In the foreground at the foot of the knoll is the guardhouse. [Marc Wanamaker] □

A 1921 view of Pickfair, the estate built by Mary Pickford during her marriage to Douglas Fairbanks, Sr. A short drive off Sunset, it is still considered a "Sunset mansion" to tourists and local residents. Buddy Rogers, the late silent star's husband, lived in the mansion until 1980, when it was sold to Jerry Buss, owner of the Los Angeles Lakers basketball team. Rogers remains on the property, however, occupying the spacious four-bedroom guest house. [Marc Wanamaker] □

BEL-AIR/BRENTWOOD
The Boulevard's Suburban Paradise

Sprawling across the shaved-off rims of low knolls — with used-brick or flagstone driveways and pathways leading from the road up to their entries — the super-homes of Bel-Air are designed by leading residential architects and decorated by some of California's most notable interior designers, who spend huge sums to please their clients. Landscape artists and gardeners, paid handsomely for their work, keep the yards and surrounding grounds in posh condition. Cropped hedges and sweeping lawns are outlined with brilliant flower beds; creatively sculptured flowering bushes and miniature trees trimmed with Oriental flair accent terraced patios and Olympian swimming pools. You might encounter a uniformed gentleman at Bel-Air's east gate who will want to know your reason for entering these "sacred" grounds.

In recent years, however, rules have been relaxed to allow a certain number of tourists to drive among the mansions. Tour buses park just inside the gates where paying customers transfer to smaller vehicles to tour the winding drives. Celebrities living in Bel-Air — Henry Fonda, Myrna Loy, Gregory Peck, and basketball star Wilt Chamberlain, to name a few — keep their addresses secret to discourage curious sightseers and prying reporters and photographers. So do many eastern retirees and millionaire industrialists, such as the Dodge family, who hire round-the-clock guards. Television's perennial host Johnny Carson has lived in Bel-Air for several years; his property is guarded every minute by closed-circuit television cameras. On weekends and nice-weather days vendors queue up along Sunset selling maps to the movie stars' homes. The maps are often outdated and incorrect — a tourist gawking at a mansion said to be occupied by Burt Reynolds may in fact be viewing the home of a well-to-do underwear manufacturer.

Some of the most imposing mansions, built in Bel-Air's earliest years, belong to descendants of a few of early California's Mexican land grant owners, such as Manuel Dominguez, Jose Sepulveda, and Ygnacio del Valle, but these homes are never pointed out on the maps. Along their drive tourists may happen to pass remnants of the great 1961 fire that raced down the beautiful hillsides to burn everything in its path. It was one of California's driest seasons and many mansions, some valued at 1.5 million dollars each, fell to charred rubble and heaps of ash. The late comedian, Joe E. Brown, ill from a stroke, had escaped his home just minutes before it burned to the ground.

Developed in the early 1920s by Alphonso Bell, descendant of an early California settler, the enclave comprises a residential area with a hotel and a country club, and three churches thrown in. There's no commercial section *per se*. At the Bel-Air Hotel, just off Sunset on Stone Canyon Road, you can indulge in the life-style of the rich for a mere $200 per night; the hotel staff welcomes visitors with open arms, in a most uncommercial manner.

You can't tell exactly where Bel-Air begins and the northern fringe of Westwood ends, where, once more, Bel-Air hugs Sunset Boulevard for a short distance until Brentwood is reached. On leaving Beverly Hills it's easy to pass into the northern fringes of Westwood and go out again without realizing it. Among the elm trees, though, as the road bends near Groverton Place, you can see discreetly placed signs reading "Bel-Air" and "Brentwood Village" — although the "village" lies southward approaching San Vicente Boulevard. Narrow winding roads lead off Sunset along the north side here, entering wooded vales and green hills where lovely homes preview those seen farther along Sunset in western Bel-Air, western Brentwood, and the Riviera section of Pacific Palisades. Humphrey Bogart and his first wife,

207

Mayo Methot, resided on the lower end of Groverton Place in the late 1930s. Actress Patricia Neal also once lived in this area near Sunset when she first came to Hollywood. Until his recent death, the world-famed American composer, Ferde Grofé (*Grand Canyon Suite*) lived here. Now Charles Bronson resides in this neighborhood, just a few blocks from O.J. Simpson.

There's barely half a mile of Sunset Boulevard touching Westwood, and on the southern side a major portion of UCLA is seen. The view from Sunset, across the airy campus to the pale red bricks of Tudor-suggested edifices, briefly transports the motorist to a bygone scene from the time of Henry VIII. The land for this famous university was carved out of the Janss acreage when it was purchased by that family to develop the Westwood section of West Los Angeles, adjacent to the old Veterans Cemetery established by the U.S. Government. The cemetery land was donated to the government by actor Leo Carrillo's great aunt, Arcadia Bandini Baker. Only a hedge-lined fence and a row of residences divide UCLA and the old cemetery.

Today the university has a three-quarter average enrollment of 31,600, including its Health Sciences Department, and new buildings are continually being added to accommodate this huge student body. The pride of the university is its internationally known School of Medicine, comprising a world-renowned cardiology department and a heart research laboratory. Its Medical Center treats thousands of patients each year, and it was here that actor John Wayne died in 1979. For many years the famous John Tracy Clinic for hearing-impaired patients was housed at UCLA. Established in honor of their son by actor Spencer Tracy and his wife, it has since relocated in downtown Los Angeles. Hollywood recognizes the University's Dramatic Arts Department as one of the finest in the country. John Houseman, the famous television character actor, is active with the department as teacher and counsellor and speaks in glowing terms of its youthful Actors Workshop.

Around a bend in the Boulevard, past the west gate of Bel-Air, is Gilroy Avenue, where the edge of the original Brentwood development once lay. But across the San Diego Freeway, which slices off the edge of Brentwood, is a "Brentwood Village" sign at Barrington Place — where local citizens claim Brentwood *really* begins. Not to worry. The scenery along Sunset at this point is so captivating that boundary lines become unimportant.

Past Barrington, on the right, sits the imposing California Eastern Star Home, a palatial structure built in 1933 to serve as the last abode for well-heeled widows of true-blue Masons. Arrangements usually made by their late husbands or families allow the Eastern Star ladies to reside in peace and comfort, as if within an Arabian prince's domicile, replete with spraying fountain, velvety lawns, and fragrant English rose gardens cared for by a pair of *Nisei* gardeners. Near the home, almost embracing a supple curve in Sunset, is Mt. Saint Mary's College. Built in 1925 and set in a pastoral scene right out of sixteenth-century Spain, the Chalon Road campus is not only perhaps the prettiest setting of any school in the land, but is the home of one of the finest schools in America. Approaching St. Mary's and located on Sunset Boulevard itself is Marymount High School, noted for its excellent art department. In contrast to its beauty, it was here that in 1857 an Indian bandit was captured and hanged from an oak tree after a small posse of Mexicans and Americans pursued him from nearby Santa Monica.

From Sunset leading south to San Vicente Boulevard lies the "village," a busy cluster of antique shops, boutiques, specialty stores, bakeries, florists, investment consultants, and realtors. Motion picture and television celebrities frequently patronize the village, whose land — as with most of Brentwood — once belonged to Lancaster Brent, a prominent lawyer who acquired it from Señora Arcadia Bandini Baker in settlement for legal fees.

Farther west, where Sunset Boulevard once ended in a traffic circle, three hundred yards of narrow, rutted dirt road swung down to an area known in 1924 as Sullivan Canyon. Today this is the beginning of Pacific Palisades. Near the site of the old circle stands the stately Sunset Boulevard home owned for many years by Madeline Carroll, who retired from movies in the late 1940s. Just past the circle, as old Sullivan Canyon is approached, is Rockingham Road. Shirley Temple lived for many years with her parents on this street, just off Sunset. Two of her neighbors were Greer Garson and Tyrone Power. Across Sunset from Rockingham stands the mansion where Robert Taylor and Barbara Stanwyck lived during their marriage. A seeming misfit lifted from the Hollywood section and dropped into the verdant Brentwood greenery, is the Brentwood Motor Inn. This picturesque motel, on the corner of Sunset and Kenter Street, is identified by a subdued neon sign beckoning motorists from the Boulevard. Oldtimers in the area claim the motel buildings occupy the site of an old farmhouse where, in the mid twenties, eggs were sold to passersby from a quaint wooden stand.

In the vicinity of Cliffwood and Bristol Circle, around the bend from where Sunset once collected all motorists and fed them back into eastbound lanes, the course now curves northwestward onto that once-narrow, rutted road —

widened and paved in 1925 — and gradually dips to enter Rustic Canyon. Known then as Beverly Boulevard, this section of the famous thoroughfare eventually brought traffic into Pacific Palisades. Of all the communities to spring up along Sunset from the old Plaza to the sea, Pacific Palisades is the last — as Sunset Boulevard trails its final few miles through low hills and shallow wooded canyons, across the Palisades mesas, to meet, at last, the Pacific Ocean.

Between the UCLA campus and Brentwood are the low, wooded, rolling hills of Alphonso Bell's "upper class tract." Scores of millionaires have built their mansions behind these majestic gates.

A chimney is all that remains
of a mansion destroyed in the
1961 fire that burned over 100
homes. □

Mary Hemingway, widow of
author Ernest Hemingway, in
1977. On her visits to Southern
California she resides at the Bel-
Air Hotel. ☐

The late Cole Lesley, friend and confidant of actor-dramatist Noel Coward, was a producer and director of London musicals for four decades and a frequent visitor to Brentwood, where many of his friends reside. ☐

Musician-band leader Peter
Duchin at a press interview in
Brentwood in 1976. □

Don Leroy Villa and his *esposa* Margaret Villa, whose great-grandparents owned the vast ranch covering present-day Westwood and part of Brentwood/Bel-Air. The Villas now reside in the coastal town of Santa Barbara north of Los Angeles. This photo was taken during a 1979 visit to the KCET Studios. □

A 1929 view of the UCLA campus. Sunset is the winding road in the upper left portion of the photograph. [UCLA] ☐

Below, a Pacific Electric bus rolls along Sunset Boulevard in 1929, passing a reservoir dug by the Los Angeles Water Department. The "lake" is still there but is now hidden from view by a high dirt bank. UCLA is at the right. On the far side of the lake now stands Mount St. Mary's College. [UCLA] ☐

Sunset Boulevard, foreground,
crosses over the San Diego
Freeway (Interstate 405) in
Brentwood. Just west of the
freeway is the village of
Brentwood. □

The retirement home for the
Eastern Star Ladies faces Sunset
Boulevard near Brentwood
Village. ☐

PACIFIC PALISADES
End of the Yellow Brick Road

Prior to the early land grants to certain of his Mexican subjects from the King of Spain, the Palisades area was inhabited for perhaps 3,000 years or more by Chumash Indians. Some were still there in tiny clusters in 1830 to 1845 when Mexico itself granted vast parcels of land to some of its deserving citizens, and then ordered the Church's mission lands to be broken up and parcelled out as well. In 1838 over 6,000 acres was bestowed upon Francisco Marquez and his friend Ysidro Reyes. The partners named the area *Rancho Boca de Santa Monica* ("Mouth of Saint Monica" Ranch); it reached from the sea eastward to the edge of Westwood and northward above Malibu from the Santa Monica plateau. Because of complex legal problems and difficulty of proof of ownership encountered by the Marquez and Reyes families, the final decree of ownership wasn't issued by the U.S. Land Commissioners until 1881. In the meantime, from 1861 when Ysidro Reyes died, part of the land had been sold off or had passed to numerous heirs. In 1883 an official partition of the land was finally approved, the Marquez and Reyes heirs receiving an equal division of what was left after several sell-offs to developers, ranchers and Mexican-American investors. The remaining land assigned to the Marquez and Reyes families was a mere fraction of their original grant.

The rutted dirt road that led out of Brentwood probably originated as a cow path, or perhaps a wagon trail, and passed over part of the Marquez land. It fell gradually down to Sullivan Canyon and then rose to a mesa later named the "Riviera Section" by one of the developers; this section is still referred to today as "the Riviera". Begun about 1921 by the Santa Monica Mountain Park Company, the newly developed area mushroomed into an exclusive neighborhood of ten- to twenty-room mansions of Spanish Colonial, Mediterranean, Early California Rancho, and 1920s Regency Moderne designs. Some of the most famous architects of America and Europe descended on the Riviera at this time, among them, Frank Lloyd Wright, Charles Eames, R. Abell, John Entenza, H.H. Harris, Tony Heinbergen, and Eero Saarinen. They designed exquisite mansions along Sunset Boulevard. One of these, Kenneth McDonald, came to live in the new community.

As the Riviera reached its peak in the mid thirties, the stylish neighborhood became a haven for European authors, essayists and playwrights, who began to sense the tragedy about to befall Germany and the rest of Europe in 1939. Literary giants — Leon Feuchtwanger, Franz Werfel, Thomas Mann, Erich Remarque, Emil Ludwig, Harold von Hohe, and Bertold Brecht, among others — fled to America, many of them choosing Pacific Palisades as their destination. Often they would meet to socialize and to read and critique each other's manuscripts. Over a seven-year period dozens of writers, composers and artists came to the Palisades to make their home, either permanently or for two or three years while they waited out World War II. Nearly 600 other writers and artists came to take advantage of fellowships established by the Huntington Hartford Foundation. Many of these creative people resided along Sunset Boulevard from the Riviera section all the way out to the heart of Palisades Village at Swarthmore and Antioch Streets. The Riviera also welcomed authors Vicki Baum, Max Eastman, Mark Van Doren, famous artist Edward Hopper, composers Arnold Schoënberg, Douglas Moore, Ernest Toch, John La Montaine, and violinist Jascha Heifetz.

England's most notable star of music hall comedy, Gracie Fields, maintained a home for fifteen years on Amalfi Drive in the Riviera while at the same time keeping a home on the Isle of Capri in Europe. Her neighbor for much of that time was

Douglas Fairbanks, Jr. A short distance down Sunset, on Tramonto Drive, lived actor Joseph Cotton, who still resides in Pacific Palisades. His home was designed and built by Tony Heinsbergen, probably the greatest designer of movie theatres both in America and Europe. Comedian Jerry Lewis, actress Joan Fontaine, and famous director Frank Borzage also lived in this neighborhood for several years. Off a secluded road, hidden from Sunset Boulevard motorists, is the Ronald Reagan residence. Built in the mid 1950s, the pale yellow glass-fronted home nestles into a small hillside lot where the Riviera mesa begins to slope. Very simple in a post-war "moderne" design, the house contrasts sharply with the ornate iron fence and Spanish-style gate that shields it from view.

For twenty-one years the late author Henry Miller lived just off Sunset Boulevard, near Mario Lanza's home, having moved to the Riviera after a twenty-year stay in Big Sur on the Central California coast. The once-controversial writer resided in an unlikely conservative Colonial-style mansion, and following major surgery in 1974, returned to the UCLA campus on Sunset to share his philosophical views with students of literature, or anyone else willing to listen. Miller, who died in June of 1980, resided on the fringe of Sunset Boulevard in the adjacent Huntington Palisades area. Nearby, an historical marker indicates the site of Ysidro Reyes's old two-room adobe, which had nearly crumbled to the ground by 1920 and was eventually demolished. Today actor Walter Matthau can be seen walking his dog just a stone's throw away from both Miller's mansion and the Reyes marker.

Sullivan Canyon, where Sunset Boulevard once ended, is no longer called by that name. Some refer to it as "the big Mandeville Canyon" but most people call it "Rustic Canyon" or "the old Uplifters area." A polo field with a spectator section once occupied the basin — the field having belonged to The Lofty and Exalted Order of the Uplifters, a sporting, social, and athletic club founded by a group of wealthy businessmen, developers, artists, celebrities, and retired millionaires. The Order's rules and objectives were written by L. Frank Baum, author of *The Wizard of Oz*. But the club is no longer active and much of its land has been sold off; the polo field lay deserted for several years following World War II. Paul Revere High School now sprawls at the foot of where Mandeville Canyon shoots off Sunset heading eastward. Sunset passes around the lower ridge of the school's campus at the foot of Mandeville Canyon Road, now a street of exclusive "ranch estates."

Around the rim of a smaller wooded canyon is the entry road to the famous Will Rogers home at 14253 Sunset, marked by a sign placed by the California Department of Parks and Recreation. This road twists and loops as it climbs to an almost hidden mesa overlooking Sunset Boulevard where the home and its adjacent polo field lie among spacious lawns bordered with azalea and marigold beds. The rambling frame house was the last home of America's best-loved comedian-philosopher-writer and his wife Betty. Will Rogers bought the home originally as an investment in 1921. He had heard that Sunset Boulevard (then Beverly) would be going through from Brentwood to Santa Monica and figured that a "piece of land" along the thoroughfare would be a good hedge against "possible future reverses." Soon after, likely for the same reason, he bought two miles of beach property less than two miles away. That was later given to California and named Will Rogers State Beach.

Rogers formed one of the finest polo teams in the country. He laid out a field directly in front of his house, at the bottom of a gentle slope a short distance from his front patio, and practiced the game every spare moment he could find. Inviting celebrities and professional polo players to his ranch on weekends, Rogers would enjoy his favorite pastime with them, with friends and neighbors as spectators. Following a match a barbecue dinner — usually ribs followed by fresh fruit and ice cream — would be served to guests outside on the lawn. The international celebrity helped serve the dinner, and unfailingly helped "clean up the big mess," as he put it, afterwards. Almost as impressive as the house itself, a large stable stands at the rear about 500 feet up the hill. He bought the barn in Hollywood and had it moved to his ranch; it arrived in two sections, and these comprise the main part of the stables today. Adjacent to the large structure is the roping ring, in which Rogers spent many happy hours practicing. For this he built a legendary reputation and many of his famous photos show him holding a lasso. His favorite ponies, Bootlegger and Soapsuds, are buried outside the barn, a testimony to the affection he had for them and for the sport in which they excelled.

The beloved Rogers was killed in a plane crash in Alaska in 1935 and his wife Betty moved away from the ranch following his death. She died in

1944, and soon after, their surviving children donated the land and ranch home to the State to be used as a park. Today it is one of the most famous places to visit on Sunset Boulevard. As a tribute to the Oklahoma humorist and sportsman, the Will Rogers Polo Club still conducts a match at the ranch every other Thursday and every Saturday.

In later years along came young actors James Dean and Robert Walker, both of whom died at the peak of their careers. They lived in ranch-style homes about 300 yards up Sunset from the entry to the Rogers property. Dean leased his home; Walker bought his and lived in it almost as a recluse until his death from strangulation. One of Walker's neighbors was Britain's veteran actress, Cathleen Nesbitt.

Here, at the top of Sunset, is where the old Marquez Road began, probably as a sheep or cow trail leading down to the sea. At the beginning of Marquez Road — which later was overtaken by Sunset — is Chautauqua Boulevard, once a Chumash trail that went to Santa Monica Canyon. At Chautauqua and Sunset, where Pampas Ricas comes to an abrupt end, stood the Reyes adobe. Now Sunset Boulevard heads in a straight line for not quite a mile and crosses the third Palisades mesa into what is called the Village — the "town" of Pacific Palisades. This tiny cluster of stores and offices is built around two main crossroads: Swarthmore and Sunset (where short Antioch Street comes in at an angle), and Monument and Sunset.

Surrounding the Village small homes mingle with spacious mansions, the smaller ones having been built by the original Methodist settlers who bought up much of the land from developers and investors who'd previously purchased it from Marquez-Reyes heirs. Methodists in the area today claim the honor of having laid out present-day Pacific Palisades on this mesa. Early in 1922 a small group of families moved into the barren area with their simple belongings and pitched tents beneath several oak trees along Marquez Road. They had been hired to survey, "lay out" and improve the general area in preparation for the impending arrival of the Methodists. Today a marker stands on the exact site where they pitched their tents. The oaks have since died, but a new one was recently planted there by local citizens to commemorate the founding of their little community. The spot is now called Founders Oaks, and sits barely a hundred feet off Sunset Boulevard.

Some of the original tent dwellers who arrived in 1922 bought small residential lots and built houses for themselves. Mrs. Zola Clearwater, who helped her husband pitch their tent, is still a resident just one street away from where the oaks stood. She remembers Sunset Boulevard as that narrow dirt Marquez Road along which, she says, about two cars a day went by. She adds with a smile, "On a really busy day, maybe five cars passed." After the Methodists built their homes Pacific Palisades saw a sudden influx of English and Scottish families. Some were Methodists, some Presbyterians, and a few English Mormon families arrived. Today the area — along with Santa Monica just three miles away — boasts one of the largest English "colonies" in America.

Writers and artists still abound in the area, but today the writers are mainly from the television industry. Also, several motion picture and television actors live in the vicinity of the Village — Peter Graves, Nanette Fabray, Louis Nye, Barry Sullivan, Ted Knight, James Whitmore, and others. James "Matt Dillon" Arness lived near the Village for several years while making profitable real estate deals in the surrounding hills.

One of the Palisades' more famous personalities was Francis X. Bushman, great star of the silent screen, remembered mostly for *Ben Hur*. Once reportedly worth five million dollars, the famous actor loved to drive his gold-plated Cadillac down Sunset Boulevard and back to Beverly Hills, where he originally resided. Having exhausted his millions by 1938, Bushman moved to the Palisades and rented a small house once belonging to a Methodist minister. He lived there quietly, making many friends and acquaintances and evolving into the town's favorite character. Following World War II the aging star moved into the home of a lady friend who had taken care of him during a serious illness. They later married and resided in her home on Hartzell Street, just three houses off Sunset. On cool afternoons and almost every evening when weather permitted, the pair could be seen strolling down Sunset, stopping to chat with neighbors, friends and anyone who cared to tarry and talk.

In virtual obscurity the daughter of a world-famous figure lived in Pacific Palisades for several years — only a few of her close friends in the world of dance knew her true identity. Her name was Kyra Markevitch, elder daughter of Vaslav Nijinsky, the man considered to be the greatest ballet dancer of all time. Herself an accomplished dancer and actress by the time she was twenty-four, Kyra Nijinsky married and divorced Igor

Markevitch, a resident of France and a renowned conductor in Paris and Vienna. Kyra reportedly lived near Drummond Street, which crosses Sunset as the thoroughfare approaches the Village. She departed the Palisades for San Francisco, however, in the early 1950s.

Upon the break-up of the old rancho, when portions of the Marquez-Reyes holdings were being sold off, a group of investors banded together and formed the Santa Monica Land and Water Company. It bought acreage from various other landowners who'd also acquired pieces of the rancho in a series of complicated transactions. Three of these landowners were Col. Robert Baker, Charles Larrabee, and the widow of Francisco Marquez, Roque Valenzuela de Marquez. Management and control of the company eventually fell to Arthur Loomis, a foresighted developer who not only laid out and built entire sections of the land over six decades, but who actively campaigned for the extension and widening of the great Boulevard in order to enhance the value of his newly-developing residential projects. Company headquarters for the Palisades area was built in 1924 at the corner of Sunset and Swarthmore, the first commercial structure to rise in the area. The company sold pieces of land to other developers from time to time and the last community along America's Dream Street evolved into one of the most beautiful sections of Southern California. Descendants of Arthur Loomis today occupy a suite of offices in the old building and continue to operate a prosperous insurance and real estate business.

A stroll about 200 feet north of the old Land and Water building takes you to the rim of the shallow canyon on which Mrs. Clearwater and the other "tent families" settled. The little canyon was known as Temescal Canyon and is still called by that name. Palisades High School now lies at the bottom, occupying the site of an ancient Chumash camp. Some of the rooftops of the school can be seen from the nearby "Founders Oaks" marker.

Beyond Temescal Canyon the historic boulevard begins to wind gently downward on its path to the sea. Edged on both sides by lovely homes and spacious apartments — many built in the late 1940s to late 1950s — Sunset Boulevard approaches a section of Marquez Road that has managed to retain its original title. We're now less than two miles from the beach. Veering slightly at the Marquez intersection where, unfortunately, the scenery is obstructed by an obtrusive traffic signal, the "yellow brick road" flows serenely toward its final resting place. Past Sunset and Marquez, where Marquez Place is reached on the left side of the Boulevard, an apartment complex looms over the spot once visited by thousands of tourists each year — the world-famous Bernheimer Gardens. The Gardens reigned supreme for thirteen years as one of Southern California's biggest tourist attractions, long before the advent of Disneyland, Knott's Berry Farm, or Marineland. Unlike those attractions, this wasn't a profit-making "family fun" mecca with rides, restaurants, and expensive gift shops, but existed on its scenic beauty alone. Bernheimer Gardens covered most of what is now the 16900 block of Sunset. Originally a mule camp augmenting construction operations as this part of the Boulevard was being graded and developed, the seven-acre parcel was purchased by Adolph Bernheimer, a wealthy importer of Oriental silk. After building his famous hilltop house overlooking the ocean, Bernheimer set about transforming the remainder of the seven acres into what he called, "...an oriental garden resplendent with oriental flowering beauty as if lifted from the Orient's bosom...." He opened its gates to the public in 1927, with free admission to all.

Bernheimer mixed Japanese and Chinese architecture, with a touch of Hawaii thrown in. With its authentically copied carvings, stonework, and railed pathways, the Gardens indeed reflected a "flowering beauty" right out of the Orient. Once inside the huge gateway, visitors beheld a lifetime collection of genuine jade-embedded screens, rare bronzes, splendid carvings inlaid with mother-of-pearl, graceful porcelain objects, tapestries, rare paintings on silk, pools afloat with rare blossoms and lily pads, a multitude of exotic shrubs, and even an exact replica of the famous Nikko Temple in Japan. One attraction was a sunken garden bordered with a unique species of stunted palm trees imported from Java. Thirty different species of California flowers blended with Oriental and East Indian blooms — each garden and structure personally planned by Mr. Bernheimer. Like the Getty Museum that lies at the foot of Sunset Boulevard, this exhibit of horticultural delights served as the fulfillment of one man's dream. At the height of its popularity, Adolph's gardens attracted an average of 5,000 visitors a week. All that remains on the site now are two cracked cement pillars and a chunk of low, cracked wall, about to be removed for another apartment project.

As it nears its end past the Bernheimer site

Sunset Boulevard makes a loop at the low end of Santa Ynez Canyon, and the ocean finally comes into view. Here, on the left, stood the famous Santa Ynez Inn, a hostelry featuring one of the most elegant restaurants in California. Little white cottages, with timber porticos shrouded in bougainvillea, led to the beautiful restaurant where diners looked out through tiny panes of glass over a petite rose garden. Inside, at dinnertime, a young caballero softly strummed his guitar and serenaded guests with old Spanish ballads. Alas, time takes its toll. The entire inn, including even the auxiliary structures at the rear, is now painted dark brown and has been occupied for several years by a philosophical organization calling itself the Capital of the Age of Enlightenment.

Separated from the Santa Ynez site by only a parking lot is the uniquely serene Lake Shrine, which welcomes visitors every day except Mondays. Although the creed of Self-Realization Fellowship, which owns the property, was founded sixty years ago in America by Paramhansa Yogananda, the Lake Shrine established by him has existed for the last thirty.

Yogananda was a mystic from Calcutta, India, who came to America in 1920 to disseminate his teachings. By the 1950s he had built a huge following. His organization first bought property on Sunset Boulevard near downtown Hollywood, then later acquired the "lake" property in the Palisades. The open-air shrine occupies ten acres with a picturesque lake meandering against wooded, landscaped shores, where strolling visitors enjoy a tranquil respite from the noise and hubbub of the outside world. The lake itself is supplied by natural hot and cold springs; bass live in its waters but fishing is not allowed. During its development as a shrine, Yogananda lived on a small houseboat and each day supervised the planting, grading, brush clearing, and other work necessary to create a wall-less secluded environment conducive to devotion and meditation. At the ceremony opening the grounds to the public, Yogananda said, "In this wall-less temple we all worship Thee, our one Father." The shrine consists of a Court of Religions, honoring the five major religions of the world — Christianity, Judaism, Islam, Buddhism, and Hinduism; the Golden Lotus Archway, symbolic of divine unfoldment; the Floating Island Bird Refuge, sheltering hens, ducks, and swans imported from South America and Holland; the boat landing, from which a life-size statue of Jesus can be seen across the lake; the houseboat; a windmill; sunken gardens; and a museum. The sunken gardens feature a sanctuary with a fine statue of the Madonna and Child sitting amid an array of tropical plants. On display at the museum is a seventeenth-century German Bible which had been dedicated to Martin Luther.

Probably the most unusual attraction at the Shrine is the *bo* tree, a direct descendant of the highly venerated Bodhi tree under which Buddha meditated to attain his spiritual "illumination". A cutting from the holy tree was presented to Ceylon's King Asoka in 301 B.C. and the Shrine's *bo* tree is a direct line of growth from the Ceylon cutting. It was presented to Yogananda by the Universal Buddist Fellowship in 1957. A short walk from the *bo* tree is a sarcophagus placed atop a simple altar. The brass coffer inlaid with silver holds a portion of Mahatma Gandhi's ashes, given to the Self-Realization Fellowship in 1950 by one of the Hindu saint's shrines near Bombay.

Now the famed boulevard takes us near its end, to the site of the old Inceville Studios, named for Thomas Ince, a prominent film producer-director from moviedom's early days. Ince, with a group of financial backers, leased acreage that included land from east of the Bernheimer Gardens down through the Santa Ynez section, long before either of those projects was built. At the tip of the Boulevard — then a rough, mud-clogged road lined with chapparal — Ince built his main studios surrounded by thatch-roofed cottages and plank-facade replicas of Early West buildings. He built corrals and barns and Old Europe "fake fronts", and invited Hollywood's producers and directors to come out to his "movie ranch" to film their one- and two-reelers for America's eager audiences. The regular access to the ranch was the beach road that came up the shoreline from Santa Monica — only the hardy would venture to Inceville over the old Marquez-Beverly road in 1919. But only a few movies were actually filmed there. Cameramen faced lighting problems almost daily as they waited for the coastal fog to lift enough to let the sunlight filter through. Ince faced other financial woes as well and abandoned the project in 1920. A few independent producers rented the empty studios for about a year and a half, but in 1922 most of the structures burned to the ground, leaving only a handful of shacks clinging to the cliffs at the foot of Sunset until 1925. A four-story apartment complex hugs the hillside site today.

Above and behind these apartments, just north of the mouth of Sunset, stood the Stretto Way homes of John Barrymore and Leon Kauffman, an English wool dealer. These homes were built between 1927 and early 1929. Kauffman's "Villa de Leon", noted for its half-dozen nude female statues guarding the entry gates, was eventually purchased by Prince Ali Khan for Rita Hayworth, but there's no evidence that she actually occupied the mansion. After two years Barrymore sold his Stretto residence and moved back to Beverly Hills near Sunset Strip.

Not actually on Sunset but up Pacific Coast Highway about a quarter mile towards Malibu, a re-created ancient Roman villa faces the ocean. Called the Roman Villa of The Papyri, it is more commonly known as the J. Paul Getty Museum. Situated on what was originally sixty-five acres of Palisades land belonging to Ysidro Reyes, the famous museum covers only ten acres of the *Cañon de Sentimiento* ("Canyon of Sorrow"), the name given it by the Reyes family. Getty built a home there for himself, but never came to California to live in it. Adjacent to the home and occupying part of its large yard, Getty opened his museum in 1954 and has since added extensively to it. In 1970 another remodeling began and today his trustees manage a Herculean-style Pompeiian edifice, seemingly lifted from the Roman countryside in A.D. 79 and deftly positioned into the low hills of the Reyes land 1900 years later. Visitors behold ancient Roman sculptures — some 5,000 years old — and can see and touch busts and filigree sculptured during the notorious reigns of Caligula and Nero, and even 2,000 years earlier when Rome was building the foundation of a brilliant empire destined to be the world's greatest power until 200 A.D. As well as owning Roman and Greek antiques the museum boasts an excellent collection of paintings dating back to the fourteenth century, and a superb collection of decorative arts, such as Regency Period furnishings, eighteenth-century tapestries and vases, and nineteenth-century masterpieces.

The southern portion of Getty's land reaches out and nearly touches Sunset Boulevard in the Santa Ynez area. Just below this point the Boulevard ends. It meets Pacific Coast Highway as that north-bound thoroughfare starts to enter Malibu. The final Sunset Boulevard address is assigned to a large gas station, on the northeast corner by a three-way traffic signal — unglamorous, unsightly, unbecoming to the surrounding beauty, an intrusive silhouette against a seascape backdrop. In this unlikely setting the great thoroughfare comes to rest.

A publicity photo of Will Rogers taken around 1925. [Will Rogers State Historical Park] □

Will Rogers rides Soapsuds,
one of his favorite mounts, on his
polo field in 1932. [Will Rogers
State Historic Park] □
Rogers in a relaxed moment
on the patio of his ranch. [Will
Rogers State Historic Park] □

Eucalyptus trees line scenic
Sunset Boulevard on the lower
edge of the Palisades near
Chautauqua Boulevard, a former
Chumash Indian trail leading to
Santa Monica Canyon. Actor
Robert Walker lived nearby. ☐

A lone car heads southeastward along Marquez Road, later Sunset Boulevard, near the Founders Oaks in 1921. The mesa just beyond the oaks is present-day Palisades Village. Palisades High School now rests in the shallow oak-studded canyon to the right of the automobile. 50 years before this photograph was taken, the land was part of the Marquez-Reyes rancho. [Zola Clearwater Collection] ☐

Below, the Pacific Palisades founders pitched their small tents and began grading roads and lots in 1922. Sunset Boulevard now runs from right to left about 50 feet beyond the pole near the center of this photograph. The "tent families" served as an advance party who prepared the area for land developers and investors. Later hundreds of Methodists arrived to build homes on the improved land. [Zola Clearwater Collection] ☐

About 60 years ago Zola Clearwater and her husband pitched their tent on Marquez Road, later Sunset, and made Pacific Palisades their home. The first among a dozen settlers in the area, she saw Marquez widened and paved and turned into Sunset Boulevard's last link to the sea. □

The original oaks are gone, but the Founders Oaks "island" in the foreground marks the spot where the Clearwaters and others pitched their tents and established Pacific Palisades. Sunset Boulevard heads westward over the rise in the background. □

An art-deco showpiece, the Department of Water and Power building graces Sunset Boulevard in the heart of Palisades Village. ☐ The beautiful Santa Monica Land and Water Company headquarters serves as the backdrop to company employees gathered for an anniversary group picture in 1927. They're standing on the grass shoulder of Sunset Boulevard. [Santa Monica Land and Water Company Collection] ☐

A busy village now surrounds the building, with Antioch and Swarthmore Streets in the rear. [Santa Monica Land and Water Company Collection] □

A corner of the Village Green, at Swarthmore and Sunset in Palisades Village. Once a "dead" spot of no commercial value, the area was converted to a small park for those who wish to pause and enjoy a summer sea breeze. □

A portion of the Bernheimer Gardens on Sunset near Marquez in July, 1939, shortly before demolition. The attraction, free to the public, featured rare plants and collections of Oriental art objects. [Los Angeles Public Library] □

Below is a replica of the Nikko Temple, the central attraction of the beautiful Bernheimer Gardens, which once brought 5,000 visitors a week. [Los Angeles Public Library] □

The Gardens were owned,
designed, and built by Adolph
Bernheimer, a Los Angeles silk
importer. [Los Angeles Public
Library] □

235

Near the site of the old
Bernheimer Gardens, Sunset
Boulevard takes a sweeping
curve. ☐

Today Sunset Boulevard winds gracefully down between these two hills to meet the Pacific Ocean. In 1918 it was a twisted, muddy road leading from one section of the Inceville Studios to the other portion at the beach.

[Marc Wanamaker-Bison Archives] □
Below, the Inceville Movie Studios in 1912 at the far end of Sunset, the washed-out dirt road running left to right toward the sea. Unfortunately, ocean fog

shrouded the compound nearly every morning, creating havoc for cameramen and preventing owner Thomas Ince from realizing financial success from his dream. [Bruce Torrence Historical Collection] □

Thomas Ince directing *Civilization* at his Inceville Studios in 1915. Ince was later murdered on board William Randolph Hearst's yacht, witnessed by Marion Davies and columnist Louella Parsons. The killer was never apprehended. [Marc Wanamaker-Bison Archives] □ Below, mud from heavy rains clogs the foot of Sunset Boulevard at Pacific Coast Highway in 1938. An upgraded Standard Station occupies the same spot today. [Zola Clearwater Collection] □

Sunset Boulevard terminating
at Pacific Coast Highway. ☐
In the bottom photo is the
highway looking towards Malibu,
just north of Sunset Boulevard.
☐

Lovely fountains grace the
main entrance to the J. Paul
Getty Museum on Pacific Coast
Highway near the end of Sunset. □

Doric columns line a portico at
the Getty Museum. The Getty
Trust maintains the museum in
jewel-like condition. ☐

Two visitors sit in the Southern California sun with a 2,000-year-old Roman youth in the forecourt of the Getty Museum. Copying formal gardens typical of Roman estates, the grounds are lavished with shrubs, vines and laurel trees. ☐

Young surfers adroitly balance on rolling, foaming breakers as they dash headlong toward the shore. At day's end a spectacular orange-red solar glow reaches down to tint the Pacific waves, throwing its brilliant hues onto bathers, lingering lovers-on-the-beach and those surfers now carrying their boards back to their cars. Having come twenty-seven miles from the Plaza where it began nearly two hundred years ago, the Boulevard has become a golden thread of history, connecting the old with the new. This magical "yellow brick road" has indeed woven the very fabric of Southern California — its people, its style, its dreams, its virtual lifeblood. Extending far beyond even Hollywood's wildest imagination, Sunset Boulevard is truly *America's Dream Street*. ☐